HOW TO OPTIMIZE ENTERPRISE IT PERFORMANCE

Abul Mohaimin
with Thomas J. Feliciano

How to Optimize Enterprise IT Performance

Copyright © 2018 Abul Mohaimin

All rights reserved.

How to Optimize Enterprise IT Performance

To: My Parents.

How to Optimize Enterprise IT Performance

FOREWARD

My real-time experience consulting for over a dozen large and mid-size American corporations and educational background inspired me to write this book. The organizational and operational issues discussed and solutions suggested throughout the text are not meant to point fingers at any organization in particular. Rather, I hoped to explain general issues commonly found in the corporate IT world that are often overlooked by the business enterprise. Eventually, these companies pay a hefty price for neglecting the mentioned issues.

My objective in writing this book is to help organizations stay innovative and competitive in the market and optimize operational performance at the lowest possible costs. Whether the company is a startup where roles and responsibilities are not clearly defined and proper policies and procedures are not in place, a mid-size company that is going through growing pains, or a large organization that is too massive to manage, the suggestions in this book will assist the organization in building a rock-solid company culture that aids in the achievement of their goals and objectives in a more definitive way.

Abul Mohaimin

November 7, 2018

New Jersey, USA

How to Optimize Enterprise IT Performance

CONTENTS

CHAPTER ONE: INTRODUCTION
8

CHAPTER TWO: TEAM BUILDING
12

CHAPTER THREE: TEAM NURTURING AND PERFORMANCE BOOSTING
48

CHAPTER FOUR: LEADERSHIP
82

CHAPTER FIVE: COST SAVING
106

How to Optimize Enterprise IT Performance

CHAPTER ONE
INTRODUCTION

Every corporate executive wants a company that runs itself, innovates, continuously improves, and has an exponential Return on Investment (ROI) increase. Is it possible to build such a company? Of course, it is. Successful organizations have built such an environment by empowering their employees through the development of the necessary soft skills and technical skills to produce a solid team comprised of strong individuals who cooperate with one another in fulfilling the company's objectives.

A company is nothing without the people who run it. While most staff members are not atop the corporate ladder, they remain the workhorses who build the products and services and carry out the processes. Every executive should ask themselves whether their employees are happy to return to the office every day. Just being present is not enough. The employees should feel that their role is important to the company and go about their daily duties as if the company was their own. Through every decision and contribution, the worker must keep in mind: "What would I do if this was my company?"

People are the company's most important asset. As such, executives must invest in them. It is crucial to remember that the people who work for a company also represent the company, including its name and brand. The workers at the bottom must behave towards the company in the same manner as the owner and executives do. How is this possible? The employees must believe and strive towards the company's mission, vision, and corporate objectives. They must love the company in the same way its founder does. They must take pride in their work environment and look forward to returning to work every morning. It is not enough motivation for workers to return only for a paycheck.

In order to have staff that puts their heart and soul into the company at every moment they are on the clock (and often beyond working hours), it is critical to build the proper team from the start. Once everything within reach has been done to build a strong team, it is then imperative to create an environment that nurtures the staff and unveils the best of their abilities. Innovation, creative thinking, and contributions to the best of one's abilities cannot be forced. In order to ensure such a staff exists, their work environment must assist in every way.

The following section discusses building the best possible team and environment that nurtures them so that positive contributions towards the company's mission, vision, and objective are a natural extension of their talents. The next section discusses methods to nurture the team and boost their performance. The section after that is about the development of leadership skills within potential leaders, strengthening the skills of existing leaders, and building confidence in employees to form strong and efficient teams. The last section covers cost saving techniques.

How to Optimize Enterprise IT Performance

CHAPTER TWO
TEAM BUILDING

For success in achieving the company's mission, vision, and objective, the business should be left in good hands. "Good hands" means having the right people assigned to the company's various tasks, or as Jim Collins says in *Good to Great*:[1] "Get the right people on the bus." If a bus doesn't have a driver who knows the location, the bus might never reach its intended destination. This is why it is imperative to apply the best methods for hiring new team members.

Hiring employees should not be rushed. A substantial amount of time should be spent in candidate evaluation using at least three criteria (interviews, references, background, experience, testing, etc.). Whenever possible, the hiring department should use psychological testing tools to thoroughly understand the candidate's personality traits. Personality evaluation is not to ensure the employee is capable of hitting the ground from day-one. Rather, these evaluations should ensure that the employee has the proper motivation and mindset to adapt to the business process in a quick fashion and that they can get along well with other team members and customers. Of course, when hiring experienced staff members who must hit the ground running, in addition to personality tests, it is important to run knowledge-based examinations, such as testing the programming capability via code challenges or assignments that test the analytical and problem-solving abilities, to ensure they have the skills for their assigned tasks.

The following section discusses a proper candidate sourcing strategy, which is the first and most crucial step in building the right team.

CANDIDATE SOURCING

As mentioned, people are among the company's most important assets because they build the products and services for the clientele. In today's competitive business environment, it is important to hire the most creative staff members available before competitors secure them. To this aim, candidate sourcing must be carried out using every available technique to get hold of the next Einstein or Musk that's looking for a job. The following methods can ensure the gathering of the best possible candidates.

Company Career Page

The company career page should be designed so that potential candidates don't feel lost or confused when visiting it; this means everyone from interns and new college graduates to experienced candidates. Many of the world's largest companies have a cluttered and confusing career page that fails to impress or assist the job-seekers by making their job search smoother. Candidates looking at such pages cannot easily search for the type of job they seek at their experience level and leave the page feeling disoriented. A personnel page should contain a short and clear message that motivates prospective hires to work for the company and easy-to-follow instructions on how to apply. A short video message can also be added that contains this information in a compelling medium that can easily reach the candidate.

Exploit Cutting-Edge Technology

When candidate sourcing, it is important to go beyond the traditional job board. While these job boards do have a large enough database of candidate resumes and makes it possible to find some stellar prospects, it also pays dividends to use social recruiting tools. The human resources department should use this technology to foster relationships with experienced and talented individuals who may not be active on the job market. Using social media, it is possible to entice these talents through effective messages. Social recruiting tools are highly visible on the Web and can be seen by candidates who are active in the job market and use the job boards to search for new opportunities and also by those who are passive, not entirely satisfied with their current job, but do not generally use job boards to search for new jobs. They are also extremely cheap to implement.

Candidate referral is among the biggest benefits of social media outreach. While a possible candidate may very well be content at their current job, their friend with a comparable skillset may be seeking a better opportunity. Also, the current star employee at a company can also have friends who are looking for employment. Platforms such as LinkedIn, BranchOut, Zerply, Meetup, VisualCV, PartnerUp, Opportunity, Hired, AngelList, Doostang, LaunchME, Beyond.com, Data.com, Sumry, Xing, Jobcase, Gadball, Twylah, Viadeo, YouJoin, Ryze, and NetParty are already used by many companies to great effectiveness. LinkedIn has an amazing feature where candidates can let recruiters know that they are looking for new opportunities. This allows companies to find candidates who are currently working yet still passively seeking new opportunities. Still, using the social media giants Facebook, Instagram, and Twitter to attract candidates is a venture not yet fully developed by most firms.

It is also important that the company's website be mobile friendly. The vast majority of young adults use their smartphones to search for employment opportunities. If the company page is bulky and unresponsive on devices with smaller screens, many top candidates will look elsewhere.

Build a Presence at Colleges and Universities

Again, the goal of any company should be the hiring of innovative employees who think outside the box. Engaging with youthful, energetic individuals either currently enrolled in the institutions or recently graduated is one of the best ways to guarantee that a company is full of new ideas. Students have a strong energy and desire to put their freshly obtained knowledge into practice. Internships and a regular campus presence can promote the gravitation of talented individuals to a company.

Job Fairs

Job or recruitment fairs are fantastic opportunities to engage with the student crowd and maintain a campus presence. An in-depth information booth can allow driven students to ask questions and get a taste of the company culture. Before these events, a solid social media campaign is critical to promote the engagement and guarantee the most talented young adults attend.

Hire Recruiters

Finally, hiring recruitment advisors can alleviate many candidate sourcing concerns. These qualified advisors give the HR department a break by taking care of the leg work. Recruiters who know exactly the type of candidate a company is looking for can guarantee that the best individuals are matched with a home where their talents will be best utilized.

IMPROVE THE JOB DESCRIPTIONS

The job application is part of making the right impression on prospective workers. But most professionals will forgo applying altogether if the company has failings in the job listings. Perfecting the descriptions of each potential position is a great way to attract the best of the best. This is an important step that most companies ignore. Even some of the biggest organizations in the world have glaring issues with their listings, and thus fail to assemble the best available tech personnel. These basic tips can help to ensure the best possible candidates see and respond to available spots on the team.

"Discretion is the Better Part of Valor"

Shakespeare had a ton of great witticisms, but this particular line has a payoff attached for those who head it. Long, drawn-out job descriptions will likely bore professional candidates. Beyond keeping the candidate reading and inspiring them to apply, shorter descriptions are also less likely to confuse the reader. Not every single detail about the position must be stated in the job post. It is best to save the inner-workings for the interview phase. A short and understandable listing is enough, with a brief blurb about the company culture near the bottom.

No Corporate Terminology

As mentioned above, confusing the candidate only serves to the detriment of attracting qualified professionals. Using big words and corporate dialogue does not make the company look more prestigious. It actually makes the company look pretentious. These terms also fall on deaf ears as IT workers want to know about the position from the perspective of technology, not that of executives. Knowing the audience and speaking at their level is a major component of effective communication. Job listings should be direct and to the point regarding: responsibilities, requirements, salaries, and benefits.

Highlight the Benefits

A full list of successful employee perks is listed in the following chapter about team nurturing. It is good to mention some of the job's benefits from the job description so potential employees know that they are to be respected and they are joining an organization that values its workers. Here, it is also important to mention information about why the job stands out compared to other companies the candidate may be looking into. What is special about this office? The people, the environment, the culture, the development potential, the clients? No matter what differentiates a company from its competition, the job description should touch on it.

JOB APPLICATIONS

Although there are many cutting-edge technologies in the modern world, as mentioned earlier, many human resource departments at large companies are still using an outdated job application platform. Such outdated software applications ask the user to upload a resume or CV in the form of a Word or PDF document. Next, there is a very long and detailed application which asks for a work history that involves every job, along with the start and end date for each position, job title, responsibilities, and more. This application also includes references and education, in terms of university degrees and certificates. All of this information is already present within the uploaded resume. As such, there is no need to include such a detailed application when the user has already uploaded their document.

When filling out applications for such companies, candidates often complain that after they complete this time-consuming process, they never hear a response from the company regarding the application. If candidates receive no communication from HR, even if it is a rejection email, they will never know if their skills, abilities, experience, and education are good enough for the applied position. This discourages jobseekers to submit a lengthy application when they believe their resume might be even looked at and they won't be shortlisted for an interview. So then, why should they complete this long application? These candidates have a valid point.

The long and detailed applications only serve a purpose for the candidates who do not have a prepared resume. If candidates are asked to upload their document in the first step, the application software should be able to scan the resume and complete the application using the information in the document. Companies should take benefit from the modern machine learning algorithms, such as natural language processing and other supervised and unsupervised algorithms that can take information from the resume and identify whether or not the candidate deserves to be shortlisted. Again, it remains important that the candidate receive feedback on their submission as well.

As stated about the company website, the application software must also be mobile-friendly. Most job seekers browse available positions from their mobile phone or tablet. If the application is not easily completed using the smaller screen devices, candidates will most likely back out of the process and the company might miss out on potentially game-changing candidate applications. In fact, nearly 40 percent[2] of applicants will give up if they are unable to carry out the application on their cell phones. No company can sacrifice nearly half of their potential talent.

Build a Better Job Application Processing System

While exploiting one or more of the best possible avenues

mentioned above for sourcing the optimal candidates, it is also equally important to have an efficient application system, either in-house or from an outside software vendor. After all of the hard work that goes into pooling the proper candidates, once the human resources department receives the application or resume, the next important step is identifying the right person for the position based on the skillsets and experience mentioned in the resume. At this stage, if the process or system used by HR is not able to select the right candidate, then all the hard work and money spent in the hiring process is for naught. This is why it is extremely critical that HR uses a very good resume parsing system that can extract the relevant information efficiently and use it to select the best possible candidate.

Develop a Better Parsing and Short-Listing System

As mentioned above, a plethora of potential candidates apply through any major company's career page but are not shortlisted, never looked at by the HR recruiting team, nor have their resume checked by the manager. It is possible that the very same resume that was ignored by the company's staff gets sent to an outside recruiting firm and the candidate gets called in for an interview and hired. Had the human resources department properly noticed the candidate earlier, when the candidate applied to the company directly through their site, it would save the company a lot of money that was spent in commission to an outside recruiter.

The above situation occurs for two reasons. First, the HR department is often understaffed and is lacking the resources to give adequate attention to every resume that is submitted to the company. Second, the resume parsing system used by the company's job application technology is not sufficient at properly parsing the resume and shortlisting potential hires.

The first, and most obvious, solution is increasing the human resources personnel. If the company has a limited budget, then it is possible to hire interns to assist with applicant shortlisting and interview scheduling.

However, the easier and more effective solution is developing a better resume parsing and short-listing system. Such an intelligent system uses cutting edge technology such as the machine learning algorithms of natural language processing.

WHAT EMPLOYEES ARE LOOKING FOR

A company must establish its brand and create an environment that fosters employee comfort and motivation. It is then imperative to attract the ideal employees. In order to do this, the company must understand why individuals choose to work for any given company. Below are the important qualities a prospective hire is looking for when deciding where to work. The creative and competitive employers on the market are also offering these benefits to attract the best of the best. So, in order to stay competitive, employers should consider offering one or more of the following benefits to prospective employees.

Salary

Money makes the world go 'round. While it isn't always the most important factor when deciding where to work, salary potential certainly factors into the final decision. Companies must keep up with their competition and similar organizations to see what the expected salary is from any given candidate. Then, the company should be prepared to match or exceed the expectations. It is not beneficial to low-ball the salary offer. When workers discover that similar positions in comparable companies earn more than them, morale is sure to falter. Instead, it is beneficial to go above the norm so that salary never becomes a point of contention among employees.

Benefits

Benefits are also considered when prospective workers are selecting a job. Employers must make their new hire aware that the company they selected has a better benefit package than similar organizations. Of course, retirement funds and health insurance are atop the list when considering benefits. However, creative offers can have a much larger effect than the expected standards. For example, a gym membership would surely garner a lot of positive attention. More vacation time than the competition is also something to consider. Some candidates may even be more drawn to the possibility of a corner office than to a higher salary. Companies should consider the needs and desires of their workers before distributing the bare minimum benefits.

Development

Beyond salary and benefits, employees will also consider internal growth as critical to remaining with a company and not seeking alternative employment opportunities. It is important to state the possibility for advancement early on. More important than this, however, is fostering growth so that employees are prepared for higher positions within the company. A company that has strong internal upward movement is sure to attract a pool of highly motivated workers who are prepared to advance their own skillsets, and more importantly, their own careers. A clear outline of promotion potential should be included in the employee benefits so that driven and talented workers feel secure in signing the work agreement.

Impact

Most of all, today's workers are looking to make an impact in their field. Sure, most individuals are driven by greedy aspirations, whether they be attention from management, fame, or countless sums of money. This is echoed by Peter F. Drucker in the book *The Effective Executive*[3] where he writes that anyone who has a great number of strengths is also burdened by a great number of weaknesses. However, an employee will also want to contribute to their company and to their field of expertise in a way that will allow them to look back on their working life with pride. Companies that provide workers with the greatest opportunities to make an impact will be sure to land the most talented employees.

WHAT TO LOOK FOR IN EMPLOYEES

When hiring IT personnel, of course, technical skills are of the utmost importance. However, beyond the information necessary to carry out the job responsibilities, there are several important personality traits to consider. The optimal hire should possess the following qualities: high energy, positive attitude, adaptability, teamwork, innovativeness, eagerness to learn, welcoming of and accepting constructive criticism, natural leadership (being a self-starter), ownership of the work, and a strong work ethic. Beyond these work-related qualities, the best workers are also honest, sincere, punctual, and diligent.

Strong Communicator

All employees, even the most tech-savvy introvert, should have excellent communication skills. While not everyone will give presentations to corporate, each team member must be able to explain various tasks to other members on the team. Speaking well is not enough. A good communicator knows how to listen and understand what is being asked of them. It is said: "A fool speaks, and a wise man listens." This is especially true when taking difficult or new direction.

Open to Criticism

Not all talented folks can handle or accept criticism. A mark of a good team member is that they can hear feedback. This is not simply nodding their head when being told they did something wrong; this is accepting it as constructive criticism and learning from mistakes. No one is perfect. More experienced team members must constantly revise and redirect the work of a new employee. Workers who are unable to hear what they did wrong can cause a toxic environment in the workplace. In this case, it is the leader's responsibility to remind the team member that they are working in a professional environment and clarify that their mistake is a great learning opportunity. The leader should also explain that everyone makes mistakes and professionals learn from them, so that the employee doesn't take the criticism personally. Team members should understand that their negative attitude can have an adverse effect on company performance and that leadership is put in place to help them improve.

Adaptability

In the ever-growing world of information technology, adapting to and adjusting based on new developments is vital.

This is especially true in the amazing contributions found in open source technology that sparked a massive change and advancement of information technology in recent years and gave businesses a lot of power. In order to utilize these new, powerful opportunities, many companies have embraced the new technologies. Therefore, the existing IT personnel must set these platforms up, which requires them to increase their skill set to optimize business operations.

There may be talented programmers who have not learned much in over a decade. These workers who are set in their ways fail to realize that a new method is often easier and less time-consuming. Also, it is important to be flexible and handle all types of work assigned, even if the employee feels the task is below them. The team's needs outweigh one person's ego.

Ingenuity

A great mind will use all of the tools available to them in order to successfully complete a given task. This means the IT workers should have the ability to understand and interpret information that can be applied as the optimal solution to the given assignment. Resourceful employees are often those who drive innovation, so this point cannot be overlooked.

Positive Attitude

Both positivity and negativity are contagious. One pessimist can wreak havoc on an entire team. Employees who punch in and punch out with a smile can make even long nights and difficult projects an enjoyable experience.

Work Ethic

Team members with a strong work ethic are punctual, reliable, and honest. They complete their tasks to the best of their ability and put their entire heart and mind into any given project. They work as if the company is their own, and as already mentioned, this is a trait worth finding in employees.

Teamwork

In very few fields does teamwork have a larger impact than in IT. Often projects are delegated to specific team members and then combined to form the larger project. If an employee doesn't play well with others, projects will never be completed in a timely manner.

Initiative

As repeated many times in this book, employees who work as if they were the owner of the company is a much-desired characteristic. This is because such employees feel the need to initiate projects that drive the company forward and take the same level of care towards ensuring project quality and completeness that they would for their own personal work. Workers who take the initiative and begin any tasks that need to be finished before they are asked can make the work environment much healthier and more productive. Self-starters are often the most innovative players on a team and are prime for future promotions to management positions.

Desire to Learn

Being content with the limit of one's own knowledge is detrimental to company growth. As new trends make their way into the technical offices, employees are asked to learn concepts that stretch beyond their own limitations. A desire to stay afresh with the ever-changing technological developments is the mark of an excellent IT professional.

HOW TO ATTRACT THE BEST OF THE BEST

No matter how good a company culture, how stable the clientele, nor how profitable the bottom line, in order for a company to remain competitive, it is important that the best possible individuals strive to work there. As tech jobs are growing ever more common and startups are springing up every day, attracting the best possible computer personnel grows ever more difficult. There are ways, however, to ensure the best of the talent pool joins a team and makes it a permanent home.

Creativity

Tech people fall under the umbrella of creative individuals, especially those who develop new software and techniques. A solid team must be chock-full of creativity to keep the competitive advantage swinging in their direction. Creative people need constant challenges and despise boring projects. When their intellect is challenged, these employees will strive with their full heart and attention to ensure the project is completed to perfection. As such, loading up the creative talent with mundane tasks is a recipe for disaster. This work can be delegated to interns or lower-level employees. Through engaging creative people on their terms, innovation is almost guaranteed. More importantly, these team members will not seek other employment at a rival organization where their minds will be better put to use.

Listening

Listening to employees makes them feel welcome. Simply ordering team members around will cause them to work at half-speed, with projects then delivered at half-quality (or less). The creative folks mentioned above have big ideas. These ideas must be heard with more than a simple nod and words of praise. They must be implemented if given the opportunity. Working under tight parameters will limit creativity. Letting the qualified team members dictate their terms might seem counterintuitive to management, but these workers can often govern themselves based on the project's potential and their vision for its success.

Understandable Regulations

Sure, rules exist for a reason (and not in the "they were made to be broken" way). That said, employees should be able to clearly understand the reasons for every rule. Any rules that are suspect are likely to detract from the workflow. This is because creative people fail to produce when their voice is squashed. Even in situations when a particular employee seeks to override an important company guideline, there is often a compromise to be made for the sake of quality production. If innovation is truly sought, then doing things better than they are currently done should be equally desired. Giving employees limited freedom that allows them to innovate and ask questions can often be the best way to manage a creative team.

Company Reputation

Every brand carries with it an image that people imagine when they hear the name. The reputation of the organization carries a big weight in drawing talented workers to the team. Most corporate executives consider branding as only impacting customer or client relations. However, surveys have shown that upwards of 90 percent[4] of candidates would leave their job if an organization with a stellar reputation gave them an offer. Every company should then strive to be that company with the successful branding that is capable of attracting the best talent pool from around the world, even if they are already working in a different company. Social media engagement, mentioned as a candidate sourcing technique, is also an excellent way to control the brand.

IMPROVE THE WORKPLACE

It may go overlooked, but the physical workplace environment greatly effects employee performance. Every office has its own unique look, which contributes to the way those who work inside the office feel about going there every day. The design of the workplace also contributes to the company culture as visitors will build their perception of the company from what they see. This is true for customers, of course, but perhaps even more importantly, it is also true for job candidates. If the place they are stepping into gives them a positive feeling, they will be much more inclined to accept the offer. The converse is also true: if the environment feels cold and unwelcoming, they can decline even the best of offers from the best of companies. As such, a well-designed location will not only keep existing employees and clients happy, it is an important element of attracting a winning team.

Engage Employees and Guests

Color schemes and furniture modernity impact how attractive an office space is to both its workers and its guests. A creative workplace design built around unique, colorful furniture with patterns and textures is sure to please when compared to the traditional formality of gray and mundane desks and chairs. It pays to think about the design as the way the employees interact with their job, as well impacting the way they feel when the first enter in the morning. Creativity in the design relates to creativity among workers. Psychologists have even written[5] about workers losing interest when they are not stimulated by their workplace.

The color schemes should relate to the purpose of the room. It would be highly unprofessional to conduct a meeting with important customers in a conference room decorated with childish cartoon faces. However, such a design might benefit the lounge or cafeteria. Research into what draws a given person to a given place would benefit the design scheme and pay for itself with more energized employees and visitors who enjoy the time they spend at the location.

Exceed the Standard Fare

Going beyond the maze of desks and cubicles, an office is more than the physical location where the work is done. Employees want more physical amenities in their place of work. This will not only make them feel welcome, but it will invite them to stay longer when difficult projects require overtime. Candidates will consider such extras as a gym, daycare center, and a parking garage as amenities to make their office feel like home away from home. Most offices have an extra room, typically a storage center or unused conference space. These can easily be adapted into an inviting facility that showcases the company cares about its workers.

In order to provide the most sought-after amenities, it is crucial to ask the current employees about their necessities and desires. Not every worker looks for the same things at their office and jumping the gun can have the opposite effected as intended. For example, building a gym for workers who may not consider physical fitness a priority could cause a rift in company culture. Or building a company gym could even backfire when there is already a fitness center near the office where most workers frequent in their off-time. Then, surveying the employees and looking for patterns will help to build the perfect location to keep current employees happy, as well as help to attract the desired crowd of tech professionals.

Versatility

Moving away from the desk could actually invigorate employees to work harder. Nobody appreciates being stuck in their seat all day. This is probably truer for the tech crowd, as they tend to be on the cutting edge of the culture and therefore appreciate a more relaxed environment. Demanding that team members conduct all their tasks at the cubicle could also be a demand for less innovation.

Workers want to move around and do their work where they feel comfortable. Perhaps a programmer is stuck in the middle of a difficult line of code. They may find that the open meeting room or a couch in the break room could assist with the thinking process. Moving around invites the brain to consider new possibilities. So, flexibility in the workplace benefits all parties.

The particular focus of a team or company should play a role in where the employees do the bulk of their work. Perhaps a team that invites a more collaborative approach would be better to avoid solitary desks in favor or communal tables where ideas can be shouted back and forth. For teams with workers who need to focus intently, private desks would serve best, with the possibility of working in an empty room when called for. Again, there should be choices, regardless of the overall layout. Employees should feel comfortable going between locations, each serving a different purpose.

Low-Resource Solutions

Not every company has the massive budgets of major corporations that allow them to design top-of-the-line office environments. Still, there are various ways to improve the workplace, even in tight situations. There are tons of unused furniture and equipment laying around any company. All of this could be sold, with the earnings being used for better, more intuitive products that the workers will appreciate. It is also not always vital to choose the most expensive products on the market. There are tons of well-designed options at low prices from discount retailers, some of which the company may have existing contracts with. Another cheap (or free) solution is allowing employees the freedom to design their workplace as they wish. Workers can bring their own chairs, tables, plants, pictures, and more to their working area and build a small nook that represents who they are. These intimately designed cubicles and offices will also contribute to an overall positive image of the company: one that says it loves its employees and values what is important to them.

CANDIDATE INTERVIEW

A general interview guideline should be made that is in complete alignment with the company's goals and objectives. Another interview guideline should be made that is specific to each department. In the second template, it is important that the sample questions focus on the needs of the specific department.

It is crucial that the interviewers don't focus only on the candidate's formal education. Instead, proven technical ability is a much sturdier criterion for success. It is a common practice in many companies that the technical interviewers ask about concepts in terms of definitions. This is counterproductive because many experienced workers don't know the book definition and know the practical side of any given term. For example, if they are asked instead about their daily workflow, these individuals could provide a step-by-step outline of the concepts in question and provide the purpose and expected outcome.

Because interviewing is such an important element to building the perfect team, the following steps and industry advice should be considered.

Conduct Interviews the Amazon Way

In a telling interview with the *First Round Review*[6] journal, Neil Roseman, the former Technology VP for Amazon and Zynga, outlined the interview process he followed to fill his team with the cream of the crop. He noted his disapproval of the top tech companies looking at meritless credentials, such as: an Ivy League education, GPAs, SAT scores, and the gut feeling of the interviewers. Roseman believes that interviewing is a skill, and one that can be designed to bring out the important elements of a potential hire: skills, accomplishments, adaptability, and leadership. The method that Roseman outlines can be applied to any organization, regardless of their size, location, or the type of services offered.

Roseman says that after every interview, the team should know with certainty whether the candidate will make an immediate positive impact within the company. In order to walk away with this knowledge, the interview must be carefully crafted beforehand and effectively debriefed afterwards. First impressions are important, but not in the interview process.

Roseman urges those conducting interviews to make the effort to break their first impression and look at the candidate objectively. The ideal hire is smart, has the right skills for the job they applied for, and can complete whatever task is asked of them.

Part of crafting the ideal interview is reading the candidate's resume and designing the questions to suit the person applying for the job. Roseman asserts that most IT professionals have no idea how to properly examine a resume. He looks for verifiable measurements of success, specifically percentages related to improving a prior company's business operations. When seeing a claim like "improved system availability by 50%," Roseman says it is very important to ask the candidate exactly how they accomplished this task. On most resumes, such claims are merely boastful lines of an individual who was a passive participant in the achievement.

Interview questions should dig into the candidate's "contributions, actions, decisions, and impact." There are three components of this in Roseman's system: probe, dig, and differentiate. When probing, ask for a specific example. When digging, follow up with the who, what, when, where, why, and how for every topic. When differentiating, separate: we from I, good from great, and participant from leader. Roseman looks into significant contributions on the resume that he can apply the STAR (situation, task, actions, results) method to. Sample questions include:

- What was the background of what you were working on?
- What tasks were you given?
- What actions did you take?
- What results did you measure?

Roseman urges against beginning an interview by asking the candidate to run down their resume. He says this tactic is only usable in such cases that the hiring managers know they won't hire the candidate in question and conduct the interview only out of respect. The best way to begin an interview is by introducing everyone in the room and setting the stage as to why the candidate was called in for an interview. Next, the candidate should introduce themselves and speak about IT topics that interest them. It is important that the interview begin with mutual comfort, so as nerves or personal feelings don't interrupt the hiring of a potential company changer.

The next stage of a quality interview is asking technical questions that can showcase the candidate's skills. These questions should relate to the person's expertise and highlight past experience. Every such question must be carefully vetted before stepping into the interview room. If a question is asked for the first time, there is no way of verifying whether the answer is satisfactory or not. Roseman is angered by hiring managers who cannot differentiate between great, good, bad, or terrible answers.

Every member of the team should work together to create solid questions and outline what constitutes a solid answer, even if these questions are borrowed from similar companies.

In this interview process that allowed Amazon to assemble the best possible team for one of the world's leading companies, writing code and asking about algorithms and data structures was vital to understanding the candidate's potential. Roseman also asked a series of vague questions to see if the candidate would ask him questions for more information. That showed that the individual could understand concepts and try to get the most out of client needs. Most importantly, the interviews conducted by Roseman were always fun. Sure, he asked the tough questions. But he still let everyone in the room breathe easily with a bit of humor and personal connections.

Perfect Technical Interview Questions

As mentioned above, coming up with the right questions to showcase the candidate's overall ability and knowledge is a difficult process. While Roseman recommends asking the potential hire to write code in the interview room, this is not always a recipe for success. Most technical personnel program alone, either in a quiet office or an undisturbed cubicle. Also, as mentioned above, asking technical questions related to definitions is problematic. Many programmers are familiar with the terms as practical knowledge and don't know the concepts like a dictionary. Therefore, IT professionals must ask the right questions, or they may let a talented individual walk out without a position in the company. Sample questions are as follows:

1. **Where do you see yourself [working in the company] within five years?** This question arrives at the heart of a candidate's motivations. Are they driven by success or money? Do they want to be a manager and have power over others? For open-ended questions like this one, it is important to follow Roseman's method of: probe, dig, and differentiate. The question is the probe. Then the digging asks for more information related to the answer. The interviewers must differentiate between a potential leader who wants to earn a higher salary and one who can drive the company in the right direction.

2. **Is programming your job or your passion?** Some technology specialists are skillful at their work but don't have a passion for it. They see their position as a normal job where they punch-in and punch-out. Once they are off the clock, coding becomes secondary or non-existent. Hiring programmers who are passionate about their field will guarantee they will take the time to learn outside of work hours. These types of employees drive innovation. They also require less coaching when the organization shifts its technology focus to another programming

language or direction.

3. **Where do you stand on quality assurance tasks?** Programmers who see their job as complete when they finish coding are often counterproductive. They bring to the workplace the wrong notion of: only coding, not testing. This idea showcases arrogance and stubbornness. Programmers are often asked to test each line of code and the logic applied in the code (a process known as unit testing). Coders who are unable or unwilling to do this will only detract from the workflow.

4. **What is the best project you have worked on? The worst?** Roseman mentioned digging into success stories after inspecting the resume. This is important, of course, because it gives the hiring team insight into how the candidate assisted in completing the project as intended. However, asking about failures can also deliver the goods because how the individual responded when things went sour can be seen. Every IT specialist has been a part of failings. The perspective on how and why the project failed will highlight what this person learned from the situation and who they blame. A good follow-up question could be: "What would you have done differently?"

How Not to Conduct an Interview

Even when following the above advice, it is possible to

slip into several interview no-no's. Hiring teams often focus on the wrong aspects of the candidate's skillset or ask completely unrelated questions. When conducting an interview, it is important to avoid wasting time and relying only on programming knowledge.

Wasting time is all too common. It is worth noting that most top candidates are being looked at by other companies. Extending the interview with unnecessary and wasteful banter or multiple iterations of the same questions or tests is damaging to the interview's efficiency. Because these candidates are on the job market, they are hoping to land a position in the desired company as soon as possible. As such, taking a long time in the interview process will delay the offering of a position meanwhile the candidate may receive an offer from another company.

Asking about code can be a central component of a tech interview. However, asking overly technical questions will result in candidates feeling they were under fire. All programming related questions should be relevant to the position and not general topics that showcase distrust in the candidate's abilities. Problem-solving is more significant to the interview process than pure coding. The hiring team should see how the prospect works in a given situation, what errors they see in a program, or how to solve a specific business requirement. General coding knowledge may not benefit all positions.

Testing Technical Abilities

Most IT interviews fail to realize the candidate's true potential. Programming coding challenges as part of the technical screening process often revolve around a basic premise that is unrelated to the business and the daily tasks assigned to the technical team. Coding challenge platforms such as Devskiller, HackerRank, Codility, Xobin, Interact, Wonderlic, FluentIQ, PrevueHR, Kaggle, Criteria, InterviewMocha, HackerEarth, Recruit, Geektastic, Mettl, Athena, Quotient, SkillSurvey Reference, and eSkill can alleviate some of these concerns. Because these systems are automated, it is still highly recommended to have an in-person interview with the candidate. However, they allow for easy technical ability tests that revolve around a sample work problem. It was mentioned that asking about general concepts fails to highlight a programmer's actual knowledge. The above-mentioned coding challenge platforms reduce the necessity of broad testing that focuses on terms and algorithms. They also allow non-technical leadership to conduct an interview of a skilled worker without the need of involving a developer in the process.

That said, developers can often play a huge role in the interview process. Only someone with knowledge about what is being asked of the candidate can provide an accurate assessment on the candidate's know-how. Imagine hospital management with no medical knowledge judging the skillset of a potential doctor. The same can be said about business managers who are asked to judge the skillset of a potential programmer. If the company doesn't have an available developer, it is possible to outsource the technical interview to one of the many staffing companies who specialize in IT. These companies understand what exactly is needed from the coder and can provide an overview based on any specific business model.

Lastly, it is advisable to check a candidate's GitHub repository. If a coder is passionate about their work, they will most likely have worked on various open source projects. While they may not have earned an income from this work, it showcases a love for programming and a drive to help the software community as a whole. Such individuals can be huge assets to an organization because they are selfless and have a proven problem-solving mentality. When inspecting the GitHub projects of a given coder, the hiring staff must check both projects worked on and complete projects that were introduced to the general public. Programmers who work on many different projects may have a versatile track record. Still, coders who were able to ship complete works know how to get things done.

Trial Period

Using a trial period allows an organization to test how workers fit into the company culture. Instead of asking coders to work for free, in such a trial, the new hire is asked to work on a specific project for an agreed upon sum. This payment is dependent upon the successful completion of the project at a standard the company is seeking. If the quality is not matched, then the programmer will earn half of their asked rate (as per an agreement before the trial) and not hired as a permanent employee. If (and for most cases, when) the coder showcases their ability, they begin working on the next assignment as a member of the team. It is important to remember that they passed the interview stage for a reason. This trial phase should not be abused lest the company lose its reputation for how they treat its tech workers. Programmers tend to communicate with their peers, and if they have a negative experience, it is sure to make the rounds in the IT community. A proper and honest trial system will benefit all involved parties. Another solution is to hire the employee as a contractor to begin with the promise of a full-time position should everyone be pleased at the project's end.

How to Optimize Enterprise IT Performance

CHAPTER THREE
TEAM NURTURING AND PERFORMANCE BOOSTING

ESTABLISH ROLES AND RESPONSIBILITIES

The first impression is the best impression. Once the right person is hired, it is important that this new employee gets a great impression about their new company. In order to accomplish this, each role within the organization should have a clearly defined outline of what is expected from them.

For each of the various job titles, in addition to the daily duties and responsibilities, a detailed list of the tools and technology they will be working on must be provided to the new hire. The hiring manager must also inform them which software systems they will be using. The team should have an up-to-date document which lists the SharePoint and network drive location of all necessary documents the new hire must read in order to get up to speed with the business knowledge. Also, the employee should know how to access the SharePoint location and other network drives the company uses.

It is a common situation in many companies that one week after beginning the job, the new hire does not yet have their system ready nor is approved for the necessary system access. As a result, the employee is unproductive during this idle time, which costs the company a lot of money. Establishing this information early will save time for both management and the new employee.

The following roles and responsibilities are found on a typical IT team. There may be some variations in duties or titles depending on the country, size of the company, type of products and services, and company culture. Still, regardless of the name, the hierarchy remains fairly similar across the board.

Chief Information Officer (CIO)

The chief information officer is a company executive tasked at heading the information technology (IT) strategy, outlining goals for the IT department, and developing a strategy to achieve the objectives. Because of the ever-growing importance of data and computer systems to the business operations of companies and organizations, the CIOs role has transitioned from a nominal executive position to a heavy-hitter with a major impact on everything the company does. Responsibilities are often varied depending on the type of organization and their vision and daily activity. However, every CIO balances the IT budget, offers innovative concepts for the technology solutions, and drives the employees towards the ultimate goal.

In most organizations, the CIO has a seat on the executive board. They report to the chief executive officer (CEO) and work closely with the chief financial officer (CFO). The CIO is a technical specialist who possesses talent in IT service frameworks and security. They also manage the team, so their ability to direct and teach employees is crucial to accomplishing their duties. CIOs must be great communicators and motivators.

Other names for this job include: information technology director, chief technology officer, and chief digital information officer.

Vice President (VP)

The vice president of information technology (VP of IT) reports directly to the CIO. Their job duties are similar, except that the VP does not serve on the executive board. They are responsible for the technological plan related to business operations, as well as implementing and maintaining the current systems. The VP must ensure that the company's networks and systems are fully operational at all times. This position also represents a leadership role in that they must motivate the employees to follow the plan that is laid out and train new workers to the current model. The VP also oversees technological upgrades and distributing the legwork to implement it.

Director of Technology

The director of technology is a common position that is found in some capacity in nearly every company. Within different companies, however, the roles and responsibilities for this title can vary a great deal. The director of technology is often tasked with: managing all technical operations, keeping tabs on the technology used in the company, ensuring the team meets project goals, establishing and meeting deadlines, system and operations maintenance, and the elimination of security issues. Directors also: manage the help desk, handle the budget and all related financial components of the IT department, develop the IT business strategy, and deal with all employee concerns, including hiring and firing some team members.

It is not necessary for a director of technology to be a master of every programming language. However, they must understand the concepts used in the field and remain on top of technological trends that may affect the organization. A good director has strong personal and analytical skills and is a natural leader. They must manage the team and also report to upper management regarding the team's progress on each project.

Other names for this job include: IT Director, Senior IT Director, and Director of Information Technology.

Project Manager

Project managers are the floor-level management and are

often the most experienced members of a given IT team. They focus on the organization of all moving parts that ensure the technical solution of each project is achieved successfully, including: people, resources, and time. The completion of each task in the allotted deadline and with the allotted budget is the responsibility of the project manager. They spend equal time with upper management and the team members, giving updates to the former and objectives to the latter. As such, this position requires a strong technical knowledge as well as management and interpersonal skills. Because they often work under high-pressure situations, project managers must remain level-headed throughout the rush to meet deadlines and any problems that may occur in production, design, and implementation of the technical solutions. One of the key elements of project managers is the ability to organize the team into their given tasks and provide adequate milestones to keep everything flowing on schedule.

Other names for this job include: project leader, project planner, and master scheduler.

Change Control Manager

The change control manager is responsible for maintaining the Change Management quality. They coordinate between clientele and the IT team regarding changes to the IT process. In this capacity, they accept and distribute any change request and reject such requests that are impossible or unrelated to the organization's policies. An important component of Change Management is the negotiation of potential down time the client will experience as the changes are being implemented.

Other names for this job include change manager and process manager.

Business Analyst

Business analysts are often the least technical people on the team because their job duties involve bridging communication between clients and team members, and often communicating the feelings of both to upper management. Depending on each specific project, they first determine what a client needs from the technical department, then they gather requirements and produce a project plan for the necessary tasks. Business analysts possess deep knowledge related to a specific business domain such as finance, healthcare, retail, etc. Regardless of where their expertise lies, a business analyst must be a keen problem-solver with strong communication skills able to determine vital information from customers before outlining the jobs of each team member. As such, they are also adept at managing, because their project plan is to be followed for achieving the technical solutions.

Another name for this job is a business architect.

Systems Analyst (SA)

Systems analysts determine issues in the business

solution, often after communication with the client, and then build a solution. They must analyze the time and cost needed for the given project or task. Proper communication with both clients and team members is vital to this role, so systems analysts must have excellent people skills. This title fuses the business operation with the technical implementation, and a good SA will be a master on both ends. As such, programmers will grow into this role after years working with the same company and understanding the operation and what clients expect from the organization. Excellent systems analysts can locate technical issues on their own through their analytical skills.

Other names for this job include: systems engineer, technical designer, solutions specialist, and product specialist.

Solution Architect

The solution architect is a critical role within the team responsible for solution development. These employees fuse technical knowledge with business and people skills to direct the company's IT strategy. Their business acumen allows them to lay out how a solution will affect the business operation. In essence, the architect lays out the plan for the rest of the IT team to follow. These individuals often present their case to both upper-management and team members, so they must excel at public speaking and in the ability to break down a complicated issue into easy-to-follow language. Solution architects plan how a company's hardware and software can be used to initiate a business strategy. Because of the mixture of skills and various layers of expertise needed to perform this task as intended, solution architects are in high demand within the modern business world.

Software Engineer/Developer

Software engineers are more commonly known as programmers. They are masters at both hardware and software, although due to their job duties, they mostly work on the software side of things. These job duties include the programming and design of software at the system-level, including operating and database systems. They are the team members who built the entire software platform and are responsible for all future enhancement and bug fixes. They also speak to clients and other team members regarding issues and objectives, so they must be skilled orators. Software engineers must be highly logical, possess a strong attention to detail, be skilled analysts, and work well in a team.

Other names for this job include: system programmer, system engineer, application programmer, and software architect.

Data Modeler

Data modelers work alongside architects in taking the business requirements and translating them into data models. These models can be conceptual or physical, the former helping to set the course of a project and the latter showcases the potential of the required solution. The models represent a specific component of the required change, such as improving how data moves between systems or reducing the amount of redundant data. Data modelers must be adept at time management, as solutions are often of a time sensitive nature. They also must learn quickly and be able to shape requests into logical technological solutions.

Test Manager

Test managers work in quality assurance, leading the team of testers who work to find errors in code (outlined below). These employees ensure that all delivered products meet the quality standards of the organization. They also outline changes that need to be implemented once the errors are found. Test managers must support a series of Scrum and Waterfall (or similar) delivery teams and outline the quality control measures. It is important for a test manager to have a keen attention to detail, excellent management skills, and have a proven track record as a software tester. Often, test managers are former quality assurance testers with adequate experience and a strong knowledge of programming.

Quality Assurance (QA) Tester

Quality assurance is one of the most important tasks in IT. If a software project is delivered to a client full of bugs and issues, the entire team will waste valuable time fixing these errors and the reputation of the firm will take a serious hit. Testers aren't always programmers, yet they understand coding and can realize mistakes and their root causes. They do, however, build test scripts that analyze the software. The results of these tests are given to the project manager, so they can distribute the necessary adjustments to other team members. Testers work on a given project from beginning to end, laying out potential errors that can be found as the project develops.

Other names for this job are software tester and test analyst.

Other IT Jobs

Other common positions in the IT field include: technical support, network engineers, technical consultants, technical sales managers, and Web developers. These jobs vary in necessity depending on the type of organization and the products or services they offer.

NEW EMPLOYEE ORIENTATION

Orientation is a crucial step towards making new employees feel comfortable at their workplace. An orientation should not be boring and full of unnecessary information. It should be a fun and memorable experience and different enough so that the company stands out from former jobs. That said, important information should be given to the employee during this time. All of the basic knowledge the new hire needs to know should be provided so that the worker doesn't interrupt other team members by asking simple questions. Orientation staff should produce a "New Employee Transition Checklist" that covers all necessary topics, including:

- A detailed list of systems, product business areas, and subject matter
- Required software to be installed on the hire's system
    - Computer and software logins
    - Access required
- How to access the necessary databases
- SharePoint and similar software access
- Project and team directories
- All company acronyms, documentation, and notes related to the work and project

"WHO" IS MORE VALUEABLE THAN "WHAT"

Jim Collins' seminal work *Good to Great*[1] discusses a shift in focus from "what" questions to "who" questions. This means, there should be a minimal focus on "what should be done?" and a major focus on "who is the right person to do this?". People are more important than situations, and the right people can solve issues even before they arise. With a staff that understands their responsibilities and job duties, the workflow is streamlined and has an automatic problem-solving regiment built-in at every stop.

FILL THE SEATS WITH THE RIGHT PEOPLE

As new employees are welcomed into the company, it is crucial that they are assigned to the right job. Placing the right person in the right seat is a mark of strong leadership. If a team member is not performing well in their given duties, rushing to fire them is unwise. This person was hired for a reason. Instead of terminating their employment in the company, it is better to determine if this employee is perhaps in the wrong seat. A strong leader will trust their employees and give them a chance to prove themselves in another position. It is advisable to change their seat on the bus before jumping to the conclusion that they are on the wrong bus. It will be clear that they are on the wrong bus if they continue to perform poorly under different duties.

TEAM NURTURING FOR PERFORMANCE BOOSTING

In order to boost team performance and keep the morale high, several perks should be given to the employees. Due to budget constraints, it is not possible for every company to offer every possible benefit. However, every employer should consider implementing one or more of the following activities, depending on the available budget.

Celebrate Success and Milestones

A highly motivated staff can be built through a thorough reward and recognition program. Beyond training employees for the skills they currently need and will need as they move upward through the company, recognizing their achievements along the way will serve as an encouragement for each team member and the company as a whole. The rewards may not be something big or expensive, but they will serve to show the employees that they are valued for their contributions.

While money serves to keep employees happy, it is often not the only factor why they remain at their job. Research[7] has shown that salary is often considered only after perks and other work-related benefits. Sure, paying the employees well will keep them satisfied, but recognizing their hard work will create a happy and relaxed environment of workers who respectfully compete with one another as to who can benefit the company more.

Some affordable reward and recognition options include:
- Gym membership
- Raffle drawing
- Competition about physical health goals
- Team outings
- Community Service
- Company Yearbook

Giving employees little afternoon snacks is also a great way to show they are valued. There can be a company sponsored vending machine where the employees have access to a supply of goodies. By using a spending card, the workers can buy a snack every day. This also helps to control the system by preventing abuse of free snacks.

No two businesses are alike, and therefore, the reward and recognition packages should be developed according to the team's size and personnel type, company budget, and other factors determined by management. These are only some suggestions, it is best to pick and choose what fits the organizational culture, needs of the employees, and managerial strategies.

Showcase Recognition on the Screen

A large TV screen can be placed near the main entrance of the building, near a food court, or in a busy hallway. The key is placing the monitor in a location where all employees will walk past it at least once a day. Beyond displaying company information and goals, the screen should have an "Employee of the Month" showcase. This simple tactic is sure to motivate the entire team.

Understand the Balance of Work and Life

While a workforce that is fully motivated to the company is to be desired, employees must also feel that their personal lives are valued. An easy way to do this is by awarding a key employee with a family vacation for good work. After months of long days and nights of tireless work leading up to a critical project release, an enjoyable trip serves to revitalize most employees and reinvigorate them for the upcoming work. Another tactic is providing an extra day off after the completion of a big project or to an employee who has worked nonstop to meet project deadlines.

"Thank You" cards also go a long way. These employee appreciation cards should be printed in bulk and distributed to employees who have gone above and beyond. They will either display the card in their cubicle or on their fridge at home and have a constant reminder of the company's appreciation of them. These cards should be given alongside small gifts that the employee can use every day, such as a water bottle or coffee mug with the company's name written on it.

Team building exercises based around an outdoor activity are also a great way to improve employee morale and get the employees out of their cubicles. Such activities can also be solid advertising for your company. If there is a regular system of extracurricular fun, employees are sure to gloat about their place of employment to friends and family. They will feel proud of where they work and know their job is different from the run-of-the-mill nine-to-fives.

Because work is a never-ending cycle of completing projects and taking on new ones, it is important to keep employee morale in mind. Productivity boosts will come after spending time with loved ones and doing interesting activities. Of course, it is often expected of workers to stay in the office late to meet important deadlines. Employees will have no problem doing this if they understand that their company gives them ample time to rest and recharge their batteries.

Flexible Schedule

A flexible schedule that allows employees to work from home on occasion is also important. For many driven individuals (including the writer of this book), days spent at the home office are far more productive than days stuck in the cubicle. There are also several perks about working from home: not having to wake up early, take a shower, get dressed, and take a long commute. The biggest perk, however, is sitting in an empty room with nobody to disrupt the workflow. Sure, working from home can also mean working in pajamas, but that doesn't mean it has to be an unplanned vacation.

That's not to say that many workers don't abuse this flexibility. In many offices, there is a running joke that "working from home" really means "not working from home." If this perk is continually abused, it will result in the opportunity being stripped from those who can work from their house effectively. It then becomes important to regulate the system through clear policies about offsite working. Everyone must follow these guidelines, including company leaders and management. If so, the process becomes streamlined and benefits all parties involved.

The most important policy should be a deadline-driven initiative. Workers must know their deadlines and the timetable related to specific hours allotted to them for completing certain tasks within the given project. For example, if according to the project schedule, a developer is given four hours to complete a program that is due before the end of the business hours that day, then the project manager should have no issues if this developer wakes up early in the morning and completes the program within four hours. Otherwise, workers will rush to complete their work even in the middle of running errands and balancing the life at home.

It is also important to remain professional when working from the home office. Of course, this means no inappropriate clothing when video conferencing during meetings. The worker should also ensure that there is no disturbing background noise, such as children or pets, that could disrupt the meeting. While attending conference calls, the employee must ensure they have good phone reception with a strong signal otherwise no one on the call will understand what is being said, which is very disrespectful to the team and a painful experience for them. The employee working from home should also remain online at all times, meaning they are available to receive phone calls and instant messages when necessary.

Workload is also critical towards a productive day spent in the home office. Managers should assign the employee enough work that will occupy them for eight hours. This is where a good technical project manager is very important because they understand how long developers need to complete certain tasks. A good manager will not burden the employee by assigning too much work and at the same time, prevent the company from wasting company time and money by not assigning enough work to keep them busy during working hours. This will safeguard the prospect of workers slacking off at home. Of course, personal emergencies can occur at any time, particularly when at home, so employees taking advantage of this perk should be prepared to login to the office network in the evening to complete work with a pressing deadline.

Don't Overwork Employees

It is common practice in many companies to hire permanent employees and give them more than 40 hours of work in a week. Some companies do this because permanent employees are paid a salary and not an hourly rate, so any additional work that goes beyond 40 hours is not subject to overtime. Other companies do this to ensure that these talented individuals don't also take contract work elsewhere. These companies then overutilize this worker and put all of the pressure on their shoulders for delivering the additional tasks. They think, "Why should I hire more team members when I know this employee can complete all the assignments themselves?" This is similar to the "gotcha" mentality. This mentality refers to: "Now that I got you, I'll squeeze all I can out of you like a lemon." However, the company does not understand that they are burning out their employee and limiting their overall productivity.

The overworked employee is often assigned various tasks outside of their expertise and is often overloaded with tasks that must be completed simultaneously. They shift between multiple business tasks on a regular basis, often related to different technology, which leads to poor performance across the board. As they work to complete the various tasks at the same time, the completed work is often of a low quality. That is not to say optimal performance out of one employee is not preferable. However, there is a line between promoting productivity and abusing a worker. The former benefits the business and the employee; the latter harms both.

For smaller companies (such as startups), delivering quality work can sometimes be challenging. This is because one worker wears multiple hats and carries the workload of two or three people. These companies are working to please their client through providing great products and services and often overpromise to keep the clients happy, but through overworking their employees, they compromise the quality of the delivered materials.

BUILD A COLLOBORATIVE TEAM

All team members, including and especially new hires, should take a strength finder personality test. One of the best examples of these tests is the ClifftonStrengths[8] assessment offered by Gallup. Such assessment tools help the company to understand the strengths of each employee so that management can delegate tasks according to what every team member excels at. Delegating responsibility is among the highest facets of proper leadership, and every tool that assists in the proper assignment of tasks and projects to the proper personnel will promote a more productive workflow. The following tactics also assist in assembling a team that works well with one another.

Hire High-Energy Interns

Interns are fantastic for bringing fresh ideas into a company. Proper training programs should exist to bring these student workers up to speed quickly. If these interns prove themselves as worthy additions, they should be hired as full-time employees. This process is one of the most effective methods of developing a workforce because it is possible to test work ethic, talents, personality, and other important qualities before making a hiring decision. Moreover, not all of a company's work requires experienced consultants or employees who carry an expensive salary. Much of this low-level work can be relegated to a lower paid intern, while at the same time testing the intern's overall merit to the organization. Many companies have a series of simple projects such as software manual testing or basic programming. Instead of filling the already loaded plate of their high paid workhorses, these companies can hire a series of interns. This saves them a great deal of money and allows them to hire motivated people who've already proven their worth.

Encourage Learning

Every member of the organization should be constantly motivated to learn new information and strategies. By creating a formal learning strategy that every team member knows about, employees will strive for further education and therefore become masters of their trade. If the company can afford it, a tuition assistance program should be initiated that pays either a portion of or the full cost of continued education. Such a program should be listed in the HR benefit package, so the employees know about it early on and are driven to spend time in the classroom. Most large companies allocate for classes and certificates in their budget. Even if the company is unable to afford such fees, the company culture should promote continued education as much as possible.

Workers who are sure they'll be promoted upon the completion of their studies are more likely to seek further knowledge. Another effective method of promoting learning at the workplace is through the formation of study groups at the company. Workers who are not actively studying for an exam should be encouraged to attend, and this might motivate them to join the program as well.

All team members should also be encouraged to read the *PMBOK (Project Management Body of Knowledge)*[9] book published by the Project Management Institution. Team leaders should distribute a free copy of this manual to every IT worker in the company. This useful book helps the reader understand IT project management and the overall cycle of software development.

Cross-Train

Team members should be cross-trained in such a way that a backup worker exists in all situations. For example, if a particular worker is out on sick leave, personal time off (PTO), or taking a vacation, it is crucial that the workflow continues as usual. This is especially important for the responsible person in a client-facing business who must answer questions and maintain a relationship with the client base. It is necessary that all urgent client requests are met in a timely manner. This is not possible without workers who can carry the workload in the case of an absent team member.

Even for businesses that are not client-facing, a cross-trained team can continue the flow of IT, which is the technical implementation of the business process. To implement the business, the IT team must constantly work alongside external clients in the form of the Technical Solution Manager of the vendor company. Internal client requests are also of the utmost seriousness, whether they come from the business' finance, marketing, or other departments. The business operation should not come to a halt because a worker is out of the office or left the job.

Work with Team Members

Lower management and project directors should not inform upper management about every small issue that the team members have. That is, of course, unless the upper management has requested such information. Instead, the leaders should take charge of these issues, which is the reason they were promoted to management positions in the first place. Upper management is focused on the large-scale issues facing a company and often do not have time to waste considering smaller problems. Leaders and managers should work with their team members closely. When problems occur, they should be corrected in a manner that helps the employee learn and improve. The success of the team is the success of the leader, not the other way around.

Innovation Portal

It is important to get the most out of every single employee. Regardless of how small the position may be, some of the least likely team members might have some of the most innovative ideas. The lower-ranked employees are often afraid to voice their opinions for fear that nobody is listening to them. Nobody sees the world from the same perspective. Employees should be free to express their fresh ideas in an environment where these ideas are heard, and the good ones are implemented. The best way to hear these ideas is to implement a feature on the company's intranet or SharePoint site that allows for anonymous submissions of innovative ideas. To promote such a feature, prizes should be awarded for coming up with usable concepts.

Brainstorming should be encouraged throughout the organization. Team members should be urged to use all of their knowledge and prior experience to devise innovative concepts and solutions that can ease the business process. Many lower-tier workers have ideas that can net the company a large sum of money and give the organization a competitive advantage over similar companies. Innovation is the only way to survive and sustain market share in today's competitive and fast-moving world.

The problem is that most companies do not have a proper

strategy in place that shows they place value towards innovation. Even companies that ask for innovative ideas often fail to deliver an open and easy system for idea extraction. A major reason for this is that employees who have the right idea and ability based on their past experience are not considered for the related project. Team leaders are unable to recognize this person's talent or possible contribution to the innovative project. Many times, these employees are overlooked simply for political reasons. Regardless of why they are not involved, the only loser in this case is the company.

These reasons are why the innovation portal is so crucial. Employees will then discuss their ideas as to how they can solve problems or ease the business process. The portal should pose pending problems and encourage everyone to submit their opinion on how it can be addressed. As mentioned above, rewards should be attached to solving these issues so that team members are willing to spend time thinking of answers. The issue at hand should be announced to everyone in the organization with a great prize awarded to the best solution(s). The company will lose nothing and gain more out of their employees, as well as a share of the ever-important innovation that drives companies in the right direction.

Communication – Confusion

Company leadership must practice clear communication,

both verbally and written. Proper communication is not only necessary in the business world; it is a crucial part of everyday life. Tasks given to team members should be clearly stated in terms of scope, requirements, expectations, and deadline, whether they are part of a large project or a small ad hoc task. When expectations are not clear, workers often feel lost and frustrated because they are trying to accomplish the manager's request while the deadline is fast approaching, and they have no idea what they should be working on. When they attempt to reach a manager, who is busy in a meeting and find nobody who can assist them in their quest for answers, the employee is in a disastrous state. All of this can be alleviated by clearly communicating what needs to be done and how long the team member has to finish this task. For experienced employees, managers do not need to explain how to do the task, but the expected task should still be clearly defined to them. Beyond verbal instructions, all tasks should have an associated memo. When important work is given out, a memo email should be sent to the associated employees so that the task remains in writing for reference whenever necessary.

Workload

Work should be distributed thoroughly throughout the available team members, along with a realistic deadline. It is the mark of poor leadership to dump work on an employee's lap without considering how much work the employee already has in their hands. Managers should know exactly what projects each member is working on. If they happen to forget, it is always simpler to ask then to assume the worker is free for new assignments.

Expect Commitment

Easier said than done, but through a combination of all of the above strategies, commitment should be expected from all employees. The importance of dedication to the team and to the company cannot be overstated. What good is building a solid team if the members will go on to lend their abilities to a competitor?

EMPLOYEE MOTIVATIONS

In order to properly motivate and nurture a dynamic team, it is important to understand what each employee is seeking. As previously mentioned, offering a competitive salary is only part of the solution. Today's workers are driven by several key factors that managers and leaders in every company should keep in mind.

Advancement Opportunities

It was stated in the earlier chapter that career development related to internal growth is a major reason why employees remain at their job for the long-term. Workers should not only be aware of their possible career trajectory but should be assisted along the way in reaching higher positions. Leadership must constantly remind employees of their career potential and also accelerate their growth through proper advice and relevant training. Not every talented team member is guaranteed an upward path within the organization. As such, management must guide their team along every step so that everyone reaches their full potential.

Stability

Most individuals plan for the future in some way, shape or form. This planning will be thwarted or stilted if employees don't see stability in their position within the company. If workers don't feel secure that they have a long-term job, their motivation is sure to falter, and they will be constantly seeking better opportunities elsewhere. Leadership must always remind their team that each member is valuable to the organization and their future is stable, should they perform their job to the best of their abilities.

Regret

Life is short, and people have a limited window to achieve their dreams. Workers who look back at their career choices with regret are sure to give less than their full effort to the job at hand. The best way to motivate team members is to guarantee that they won't be disappointed in themselves later in life. Leaders should share their success stories with the team and remind everyone of their humble beginnings. Talented people often look at their bosses with contempt because they feel deserving of such a high position. Instead, management can mentor and encourage workers through their own failures and successes. This way, everyone can envision a brighter future for themselves, in a bigger office with a higher salary and more respect.

Contentment

This motivation can be restated as happiness. However, happiness is linked to many outside factors, often unrelated to work. Nevertheless, contentment in the workplace is a key motivator and promotes positivity throughout one's personal life as well. Nearly everyone has experienced bouts of taking their jobs too seriously. As such, leaders should build a fun and friendly workplace where everyone can relax after the tasks or projects are completed. Team leaders should also speak to their workers about job satisfaction whenever possible. Sure, most employees will lie about being happy just to save face or save their job. But if leaders have a strong rapport with their subordinates, the lower-ranked workers will feel comfortable speaking the truth. Happiness at work means that all jobs are completed with a smile. Work completed with a smile is sure to be top quality.

PROJECT-BASED WORK APPROACH

All of the project's major needs must be identified so the project can begin with a clear objective, measurable milestones, a deadline, and an expectation of results. This is done through the implementation of a project charter and project plan.

Project Management

Poor management demotivates employees. Therefore, all IT project managers and team leaders should be knowledgeable and experienced regarding all technical elements of the projects they assign. It is common that project managers without a strong technical knowledge must rely on their developers' word, even if they don't know if what the developer is saying is true. As mentioned earlier, this is particularly evident with time estimation. For example, developers can provide an estimate of eight hours for a task that can easily be completed in four. A non-technical manager might sign-off on the eight-hours of work and pay the developer for an extra four hours while the company and loses half a day's work. This is one of the major reasons why the overall operating cost of IT can exceed expectations.

Meetings

The majority of business meeting invitations are sent without an agenda. This leaves most of the attendees confused about the content of the meeting, why there were invited, and what is expected of them. For this reason, an agenda is of critical importance. The agenda does not have to be extremely detailed. Often, a short document listing the purpose and objective of the meeting, with bullet points of discussion, and an expected outcome is much more effective.

Leaders should arrive to the meeting several minutes early. This is especially true if they are expected to present a PowerPoint or a visual presentation. Arriving early gives presenters time to make sure that all computer, projector, and audio hardware is working correctly. Doing this during the meeting will waste time of the other meeting attendees, who may be working on tight deadlines.

The meeting chair should begin by stating the purpose of the gathering, discussion points, and the expected outcome, as listed on the agendas that every attendee has in front of them. Also, each member of the meeting should be addressed directly as to what is expected of them, so that nobody feels left out, confused, or like they are wasting time. Most importantly, every meeting should end with a clear decision made the group and approved by the leaders. Meetings that end without any decision will damage the morale of all in attendance and turn them off from the productivity of future meetings.

In order to monitor the work progress and keep team members energized, leaders can call for a 15-minute stand up meeting to touch base with all team members, discuss roadblocks in task or project completion, assign help to solve these issues, give general direction, and issue reminders about the short-term expectation for the given day. In general, short meetings should last around 30 minutes. Long meetings should not exceed one hour in length.

After the meeting, an email must be sent to all attendees and associated people who were not in attendance. The message should include meeting minutes with every covered discussion point and the meeting outcome. When sending such a message, it is important to remember the business etiquette of emails. That is, they should have a clear and concise subject and a detailed body.

Project Lessons Learned[10]

Every project, no matter how successful, has failings that the management and team members can learn from. Regardless of how well a project is planned and laid out in the conception phase, there are always unforeseen circumstances and events that can thwart expectations, lead to delays, or cause a project to go off the rails. Instead of looking at these failings as negative experiences, with the proper perspective and note-taking, they can become learning experiences for everyone involved.

Lessons learned should be logged throughout all stages of the project to save time as the project moves along. Once the project is completed, these lessons can be finalized during the project closing phase. This way there is a guarantee that every lesson is accurately recorded. Management should keep track of each thing that went well, didn't go well, and why. This initiative may seem counterproductive, as the goal should always be to drive forward to the next project. However, keeping track of every positive and negative about each project will ensure that there will be less headaches and setbacks in future projects.

For issues unresolved during the project development stage, management should produce as assembly of preventative measures to alleviate similar concerns in the future. For example, they can ensure employees don't skip important elements of the development phase or purchase tools to make the workflow easier and faster. Other predevelopment improvement steps that can be taken from lessons learned throughout project development include the production of document templates that can be used for similar projects, process checklists to guide developers through important development procedures, and lists of workarounds and shortcuts that were discovered during the development of a particular project.

As customer service is of the utmost importance to large companies, these lessons can also be used to assist the technical support team. With a record of how common issues were solved during past projects, the customer service staff can easily troubleshoot technical issues over the phone or via email. This will save time but also help the company save money by not allocating resources to solving problems that were already faced by the team.

The final step of collecting lessons learned is building a best practices record. This collective list of the methods that have proven most successful for given tasks is crucial towards giving a company the competitive advantage. The best, fastest, and most effective way the team has been able to accomplish an important task should be assembled and incorporated into the company's policies and procedures. This best practice repository should also be easily accessible to all staff members, such as being placed on the database, intranet, or within company literature. The intellectual assets of best practices allow the company to continue onward at the same level of quality even in the face of the firing, quitting, retiring, or laying off of staff members and the exiting of contractors. They allow the company's accumulated knowledge to remain within the company and not walk out the door when employees leave.

CHAPTER FOUR
LEADERSHIP

Building leadership qualities is an entire topic within itself. Many great works have been written on the topic, including the widely-read manual, *How to Win Friends & Influence People*[11] by Dale Carnegie. Instead of dealing with the concept as a whole, this chapter will highlight leadership as it relates to the world of corporate IT.

Success is next to impossible without proper guidance. Having the wrong leaders in place in the IT field leads to all sorts of disastrous results. Leadership is a like a glue that holds the entire team together and also like a fragrance that envelops the entire team with a positive odor. Training and empowering leadership is imperative to accomplishing company goals. In order to know a good leader, one must be able to recognize bad leadership.

Bad leaders are insecure. They lack confidence because of

inadequate skillsets. Out of fear of losing their own position, they do not work to mentor and nurture their dynamic team members to bright out their maximum potential. In insecure leader feels that if his dynamic subordinates absorb everything he knows, then these team members will soon replace him. This could not be further from the truth. Knowledge is the only thing that does not reduce the more it is spent. A manager who is confident, resourceful, and has a strong relationship with upper-management should feel secure in their job in such a way that no matter how talented the team members are, there is no fear of being replaced. Instead, because developing a talented team is crucial to the business, credit for doing so will fall onto the leader and they will be rewarded, not punished. A leader who develops a strong team should expect a pay raise and promotion, not being booted out of the company for the younger employee to fill their chair. A bad leader who is intimidated by their team and in a constant worry over losing their job is a selfish employee who is detrimental to company success. These types of managers will recognize threats in their organization and look for mistakes in their work that can be brought to the attention of upper management. It is unnatural to be flawless, regardless of how smart or talented any given individual is. Good managers correct the mistakes of their team members to help them learn, not expose these flaws to the rest of the organization and belittle the person who made them.

LEADERSHIP QUALITIES

Now that bad leadership has been dealt with, the following are marks of a good leader in the IT field.

Team Building and Neutrality Bias

A successful manager is above all influence. They are able to look at employees based on their skills and bring the most out of them, regardless of personal feelings. This means dropping their personal ego and looking at employees free of racial, religious, or political biases. These feelings should be completely separated from the decision-making processes related to team building and management.

Look Out for Team Members

Real leaders are able to blend in with their workers and build a level of comfort. If the leader does not care about their team members, there is no way that the team members will care about the leader. Sure, employees might carry out commands in order to protect their job and keep their paycheck (because everyone has bills to pay). However, without a strong connection between leadership and employees, the workers will not put their heart and soul into their tasks. They will never innovate or conceive creative solutions that will make the entire team shine with praise throughout the company. It is impossible to force employees to be innovative, creative, or make a difference. This is the same as not being able to force a teacher to teach or a poet to write a poem. These actions must be a natural extension of an individual who wants to do them. When team members love their job and feel comfortable around their manager, continual innovation is to be expected.

Military Leadership

When it comes to the application of leadership based on discipline, a military-style leadership system with a strong chain-of-command is beneficial to large organizations. The previous point mentioned employees loving their manager, however respect is also important. Discipline follows respect, and respect is earned, not given. When it comes to discipline, there is no better example of subordinates following their leadership than the military.

Obstacle Detection

A good leader makes the effort to identity any obstacles that deter their team from performing at their best. Such obstacles include: hardware issues, software access, lack of skill, insufficient training, unclear or absent requirements, or team members lacking business understanding. Political anarchy among team members is often a cause for many dilemmas, so leadership must be very clear in directives and delegation of duties.

BUILD A GOOD COMPANY INTO A GREAT COMPANY

It is important that a leader never allows the company's employees to slip into a "happy-go-lucky" mode. This can occur when organizations continue to grow, and leaders then fail to activate employee momentum towards achieving goals and company objectives. When leaders fail to take measures to boost team performance during both good and bad times, employees lose morale and become unproductive. As a result, enterprise resource utilization becomes harder to manage.

Growth occurs in such waves that different departments continue expanding its team members and work in silos. Each team hires software developers with similar skillsets in redundancy, so that similar work efforts are being done in silos that causes a redundant work effort and poor enterprise resource management. The redundant hires with similar skills that were absorbed by the various teams will remain busy during the project development phase but unable to fill their timesheet during slow periods. This amounts to a huge waste of money with countless employees collecting a paycheck for doing nothing. This problem can also occur with expensive IT contractors that the management is afraid of losing because of their talent and value. In such situations, the manager must go around the company asking if there are any other projects to occupy the contractor who has downtime so that they can remain within the organization. The manager must ensure the utilization of this contractor who would otherwise be sitting idle and wasting company money. Either that, or they would have to let them go and lose a valuable talent. Hiring and firing costs money because every new employee must be brought up to speed.

The best solution for this problem is a centralized technology solution for the entire company. Companies should build a central application development, central quality assurance, or central software testing team that is skilled in all the technology used by the business and can be utilized in different project teams throughout the organization as needed. In this way, redundant hires can be reduced, and money can be saved by abandoning the hiring, firing, and rehiring cycle found in the IT department of many organizations. This centralized system is also possible for the project management and business analysis teams, as well as all other relevant IT titles.

ORGANIZATION CULTURE CHANGES

Changing the culture of an organization is never easy. This is worsened when cultural diseases have festered within the company for years and grown into chronic symptoms. It is very hard to get rid of these diseases because they become part of the employees' work habits and second-nature. Again, this reflects the "happy-go-lucky" situation that occurs when employees are comfortable with what they have and what they do. These employees have no drive and no intention to innovate, try something new, or even change their work habits. They will frown at any attempt to adopt anything better and more efficient. They are unwilling to learn anything new because it may be difficult for them and they feel that the old way is working just fine. They are wrong in this, as the old way was not working if it led to complacency. Complacency produces a slow, manual effort that is inefficient and erroneous. Even if such employees are aware that the new way may be better, they are afraid to change because of this inbred laziness and an insecurity that they may flounder under change.

How to Drive Change

The leader driving such a positive cultural change must be brave. They will be on their own against an entire team. This is very tough because employees will provide much push-back, start to hate the manager, team up against the leader, speak behind their back, not cooperate under directives, and make the implementation of these changes difficult at every turn. However, a steadfast leader can change the minds and hearts of even the most stubborn of employees.

It is important to have upper-management on the side of these changes. For successful implementation of this, these executives must first understand what the changes are and how they will benefit the organization. If upper-management understands, they will support the team leader and make sure the team members know these changes must be implemented. To have complete support from the higher-ups, they should see viable examples of successful changes of a similar nature. People like to see something in action before they agree about its benefit.

CRITICAL BUSINESS DECISION-MAKING

Company data represents money in today's world. As such, the important data should be well-protected so that market rivals and competitors have no chance of getting their hands on it. Beyond the monetary implications, data also contains sensitive customer information such as personally identifiable information (PII). If this data is easily accessed, hackers can trace it back to an individual at great potential harm to that person. Other sensitive data includes: biometric data, medical information, personally identifiable financial information (PIFI), and unique identifiers that include passports and Social Security numbers. Identify theft is a real threat for the disclosure of such information, but even if they avoid such heavy attacks, customers will be aggravated to have their personal information leaked that they would prefer to keep private. As such, PII should be encrypted both in transit and at rest.

Continuous Improvement

Continuous improvement is possible in the overall business process optimization. For each successful project, the lesson that the team members learned should be collected. For project failures, the corrective action should be identified so that it can be applied in the future. As such, there are no failings, only learning processes that help everyone on the team grow into better employees.

Variance Reduction

Automation should be encouraged in the appropriate business practices. This will save time and allow team members to focus on difficult tasks rather than spending energy and resources on easily completed work. Automation is possible through the fine-tuning of existing processes, roles, and responsibilities.

Documentation

Failure to document is an evil practice, but one that is wide-spread. All leadership and IT workers realize the importance of documentation. Still, it is neglected because of lack of time, laziness, or employees who feel insecure that they might be fired. As such, these types of employees never document their work. Such team members may feel that if they document their business project and work, then they can easily be replaced by a new employee who can come in and pick up the job quickly by reading through the documentation. However, these insecure employees do not understand that no one in this world is indispensable.

All tasks, business requirements, business rules, functional designs, technical designs, programming works, analyses, test plans, test cases, testing processes, and tests should be documented in such a way that it can be easily reproduced by every member of a given team. While programming, in-line documentation must be performed so that any future developer can understand the program and perform necessary edits, updates, or upgrades. It is even possible that the developer who wrote the initial program could forget a part of it because they worked on it years ago. All necessary documentation must be carried out as the program is being developed. This is true for any artifact in the software development lifecycle that was mentioned above.

Save to Network Drives

All work should be saved on network drives in the team directory, respective business area, or project directory. Nothing should be saved on local systems. In the case of system crashes that destroy the local drive, all the valuable data is lost. This is also true is a virus or hack takes over the system. Backing up to the directories is an easy solution against hardware failures destroying projects and setting the workflow back.

SOFTWARE AND DATA QUALITY

As silly as it sounds, the importance of quality is often undermined by company leadership because of time and cost. They urge team members to finish projects quickly, at minimal cost, so the project can be pushed out the door and they can move on to the next one. This mentality has a serious detriment to the company's reputation and can destroy customer relationships. This can easily be seen on a smaller scale when purchasing goods. Anyone who receives a poor-quality product or service from a shop will be hard-pressed to return to that location. When purchasing from Internet megastores like Amazon, people don't normally take the time to write a positive product review. However, if the product is of poor quality, they will not only return the item to the seller, but they will write a scathing, negative review. As such, quality should not be taken lightly.

Quality assurance is as important as fast, cost-effective project completion. All jobs, large or small, must be peer-reviewed. Large development projects must be properly tested using the organization's testing methodology. No deliverables should ever leave the company before undergoing proper testing.

Many small organizations provide IT solutions to large organizations and over-promise an unrealistic expectation within the deadline. In order to deliver extra features, developers will then work day and night, working many extra hours and compromising their sleep. They also compromise quality in this regard because such a work schedule is sure to induce an error-filled product. Instead of falling into this situation of promising beyond what is reasonable for the IT team, it is important to have a strong relationship with the client so that realistic deadlines can be set that allow for proper testing before final delivery.

"GET THE WRONG PEOPLE OFF THE BUS"

Returning to Jim Collins' running bus metaphor from *Good to Great*[1], it is important for company leaders to "get the wrong people off the bus." Everyone has bills to pay, and therefore, must work to earn money. However, the business world is one of practicality, of dollars and numbers. There is no room for emotion when the organization has a bad apple. Leaders must make the hard choices and fire people who are not working out.

Sure, a manager must make and implement these difficult decisions that involve people's lives and must remain steadfast when doing so (not being swayed by an emotional response). However, this does not mean this process must destroy the worker forever and leave them with a long-term stain of being a cancer within an organization. It is also important that the one being removed leaves with positive feelings about the company. After a leader tried their best to work out a developmental plan with the team member that did not work out and made the decision to let that team member go, it must be done with grace and respect. Letting people go with grace is the mark of a true leader. Nobody wants to be caught up in an employee firing that leaves devastation in its wake, either during the exit-stage or in the aftershock. A good manager will explain to the employee, truthfully, why they are being let-go. But they will also remind them that it the decision was not about personal feelings. Beyond this, the leader must go back through this employee's hiring process and find mistakes in the vetting process that will assist the hiring of future employees.

EXIT INTERVIEW

Appointing the wrong leadership can have disastrous results. When leaders are promoted who lack managerial skills, this leads to discontentment from employees, and eventually, the departure of quality personnel from the company. Leaders must be able to show appreciation to their team members, effectively communicate the company's vision and strategy, and build a team that is committed to the company's success. Retaining employees is important because it has been proven that higher turnover relates to lower overall performance. As such, conducting exit interviews is crucial so that the organization can understand why its top performers stay, leave, and what changes these former employees would have liked to see been implemented.

Why Exit Interviews Fail

There are two major reasons why the few companies who do conduct exit interviews walk away with less than sufficient data that can assist in increasing employee retention. The first is that employees who are leaving a company will be less than honest during this interview. There are a number of reasons why they may not express their honest feelings: maybe they feel afraid to express dissatisfaction with their management for fear of losing references, they can feel pressured to say what the company wants to hear, or they may simply feel unmotivated to tell the truth to a company they feel has failed them.

The second major reason relates to the overall exit interview strategy itself. This means the company does not have a consensus of best practices as to how to go about the interview and what to gain from it. The goals, strategies, and implementation of these exit interviews are not fully realized because there is a lack of guidance as to what they represent and why they are important.

Exit Interview Goals

A properly implemented exit interview strategy should highlight employee thoughts, reveal issues within the organization, and give management insight as to where the company stands in the landscape of similar organizations. As outlined by a piece in the Harvard Business Review, effective EI programs must focus on the following six goals.[12]

1. **Expose HR Problems:** As mentioned in the above sections, employee motivations revolve around more than salary and benefits. Most companies place too much focus on these two points during the exit interview and ignore the glaring HR issues that force an employee out the door.

2. **Recognize How Employees See the Work:** Management should gain valuable data during the EI about employee perceptions of the company culture, their working conditions, their responsibilities, and relationships with coworkers.

3. **Understand Effectiveness of Management:** This allows the organization to locate the effective managers who are worth rewarding and uncover the failing managers who are damaging the company. Viable outcomes of this goal should be to develop better management training programs and promote people into managerial roles who fit the winning criteria.

4. **Discover HR Compensation of Competitors:** Beyond discovering the salary rates, benefit packages, offered vacation time, and advancement opportunities of the competition, exit interviews also give management the

chance to see what companies are stealing their valuable employees and why.

5. **Gain Ideas to Improve Company Innovation:** More than determining why the employee is leaving, an effective exit interview should also highlight what the company is doing wrong. When innovation is the ultimate goal of a successful and constantly growing organization, a potential question to ask departing team members should resemble: "Complete this sentence: 'I don't understand why the company doesn't...'" The trends that emerge from such a question could help the company in untold ways.

6. **Ensure Former Employees Vouch for the Organization:** Finally, the employee on their way out the door should not leave with a sour taste in their mouth. If the exit interview treats this former team member with dignity, they can continue to recommend their friends to work for this company. They could even serve as an ambassador of their former workplace at their new job, which is nothing but free publicity.

Exit Interview Strategies

A major issue with most exit interviews is that they are led by the human resources department. The problem with this is that such interviews rarely develop into furthering the company's strategy for success. As such, it is important that these interviews be conducted by the second or third-line managers with a strategy related to design, implementation, and analyzing results carried out by the executive committee. Second-line managers work best because they are one step away from the employee, and as such, are much more likely to receive honest answers from the departing employee. Post-departure interviews can also be carried out by a consulting firm. Because of their lack of bias due to no prior relationship with the company or former employee, these consultants are much likelier to generate usable information.

Who is interviewed upon departure should also be carefully considered. Some companies make it a point to conduct exit interviews for everyone out the door, whilst others focus on professionals and executives, or employees who showcased high potential. Targeting higher-end personnel works best, as they are the team members harder to replace. They will also continue to hold dominant positions in competitive organizations throughout their career, so they are the best possible candidates to become ambassadors for the organization.

It is also best to conduct these exit interviews at the midway point between the employee giving their notice and them finally leaving the organization. When the employee is in their final stretch at the organization, they are likely to be mentally checked out and interviewing these individuals would provide little useful information. Exit interviews can also be effective if they are carried out around a month after the professional has left. This is because there is much less pressure on them and they are likely to respond honestly about the failings that caused them to walk away. This can assist with building programs to prevent talented workers from leaving in the future. The timing all depends on the management style and type of company, but it is best to avoid interviewing too early or too late. It also depends on whether the organization has a policy of one or multiple exit interviews. If multiple interviews are better suited to the organization, then the final one should be conducted between three and six months after the employee has left.

    One of the most crucial elements to conducting interviews is fusing a prepared questionnaire with spontaneous, unplanned questions. The questionnaire is helpful towards noticing trends that can be more easily analyzed in the future. When asking questions without a structure, the interviewee will elicit more natural, unexpected answers that can also be helpful towards finding issues within the organization that can be addressed.

    The way the interview is conducted also contributes a great deal to the usability of the results. The interviewers should be patient, talk less, and listen more. They should not display authority in the interview, but rather come across as friendly and welcoming. It is also important not to discuss plans to solve the departing employee's concerns, but rather ask them how they would fix the issue. The departing employee should never be embarrassed in the interview either. They should be asked what they liked about their jobs, what they disliked, and how their peers viewed their contributions to the company. It is important that all questions are only asked to provide verifiable data that can be used to help the organization improve, not to compare the former company with the job they are going or ask about personal issues.

How to Use the Obtained Information

Once the information from the exit interview is collected, the management team related to the interview process must first consider the sensitivity of the answers received. It is important that honest remarks given in the interview room be respected, especially with relation to current employees and executives. As such, distribution of the obtained information should protect the interviewee so that current employees know the company values privacy and are not afraid to speak their minds with candor should they leave the organization and be called for an exit interview themselves.

The data should also be presented based on a specific timetable in a manner that allows the company to grow from the feedback. For example, a senior line manager may present exit interview related to their former subordinates at an executive committee meeting. More than presenting the data, such meetings should also brainstorm how the organization should respond to the criticisms. If no action is to be taken based on the answers received, then reasons why this issue is not being resolved should also be presented.

USE CUTTING-EDGE TECHNOLOGY

Once the right team members are hired, they are given the right environment to grow, they were nurtured in such a way that they produce innovative products and services, it is crucial that the team is given the right tools to work with. It is common for most mid-size and large organizations to base the software, tools, and technology used in the company on what the competitors or using or on the current trends. In order to gain a competitive advantage, leaders must predict the market need ahead of time. As such, leaders must constantly read technology journals and keep their eyes on the innovative companies in Silicon Valley. Sure, there are competitive companies in other locations, but the companies in Silicon Valley have a proven record of inventing or early adoption of the most recent cutting-edge technology solutions. Leaders must be aware of the new and upcoming technologies being used in other parts of the country and across the world and make use of those technologies before the competitors do. Through adherence to the following tips, leaders can be trend-setters and remain competitive in the ever-growing technology market.

How to Use Technology to Improve the Organization

Technology has rapidly changed in the last few decades, but there is no bigger change than the constantly-online trend sparked by smart phones. For companies to remain competitive in today's market, they must shift their focus towards the online technology and make it part of their everyday business operation. There are a number of methods leaders can implement using the Internet to improve the company's productivity.

The first is to showcase to customers and clients that the business possesses a tech savvy mentality. The company's online presence should be "cool," which means having an up-to-date website that meets the standards of leading organizations. Beyond building a stellar site, leadership should also implement digital marketing to ensure that this cutting-edge home base for the organization and its offerings is found by the intended people.

Within the company itself, there are a great many applications and software tools that can improve the daily workflow. For example, managing the company projects, tasks, and necessary activities can be managed with a simple app like Todoist. These applications also sync to the calendars of the relevant personnel, so there are always reminders of what work needs to be done and by when.

There are also software applications that can ease with the payroll and bookkeeping needs of the organization. Most major organizations rely on payroll apps to increase the productivity of distributing checks, making direct deposits, and filing their taxes electronically. Bookkeeping technology allows for the organization of all the organization's important documentation, invoices, deductions, expenses, and other financial services. Staying afresh with these offerings can reduce overall accounting costs a great deal and make everyone's lives much easier.

Remaining in the Loop of Technological Trends

As mentioned above, leaders should always be on top of the latest technological happenings so that the organization is moving ahead with the times. For small businesses, this may be difficult, because they are less likely to adopt new technology and stick with the methods that have proven successful in the past. However, if competitors are using the latest technology in their operations, this only means that companies that drag their feet when accepting new technology will be left behind. Leaders must then remain on top of these trends through constantly educating themselves.

This means that leadership should always engage with the technology journals, blogs, websites, and books to read about what is happening and find technological solutions that can improve their company. Beyond learning about the latest developments, reading these sources on a regular basis will also give leaders insight as to how similar organizations are using these new technologies. Then, leaders should make an inventory of the company's needs, failings, and where they fall behind respective of the trends, so that they can make a plan to implement some of this cutting-edge technology in the daily operation. It is best not to jump into acquiring all of the latest gadgets and software without doing the proper research as to what others are saying about them and how they are being used in similar organizations.

Necessary Technology to Implement

Staying afresh with all the latest technological trends can feel overwhelming at times. Fortunately, not every technology is suitable for every business type and size. However, there are several key technological solutions that every business that wants to remain competitive should already be using.

The most obvious of these solutions is the usage of cybersecurity systems. As repeated throughout this work, data is the company's second most valuable resource, second only to the personnel. The loss or corruption of this data can cost companies untold sums of money due to loss of customers once their personal information is revealed and their trust is broken. Verizon reports[13] more than 60,000 cyberattacks at major companies each year, which makes the implementation of the best possible cybersecurity system crucial.

Another obvious technology that every business should use is outreach through the free social media applications. This allows any company to communicate with customers and clients directly and reach a massive portion of potential customers across the globe. These platforms are easy to run and operate, so every single organization should have social media specialists working for them.

Another easy solution is the implementation of cloud services to consolidate all business documentation and communication onto one platform. More than storing data, cloud can be used as an all-inclusive database that allows every member of the team to collaborate on a given project. Cloud represents a larger landscape than the personal platforms used by laymen on mobile phones and for simple file sharing, with a great deal of cloud services available that are more suitable to businesses.

CHAPTER FIVE
COST SAVING

The cost of running the IT operation weighs heavy on the budget of any organization. CIOs and other members of management work hard to deliver these vital business functions whilst keeping spending as low as possible. It is difficult for most companies to cut IT costs because the components related to managing technology and technological solutions, such as personnel, hardware, and software, are often unmovable. Or at least, that's how they appear. The following section addresses cutting costs where applicable and saving the organization money through easy-to-follow steps.

COST SAVINGS BY PEOPLE

The price of workers contributes to a huge chunk of IT spending. However, it is possible to deliver the same output and reduce the need to hire talented professionals who come with a heavy price tag. Sure, any organization wants the best possible employees on their team. Still, there are viable workarounds to getting quality output with a strong talent pool and minimal spending.

Interns

As mentioned in the section about team nurturing, interns bring fresh ideas and a youthful work ethic into any organization. They also reduce spending, because it is possible to hire a plethora of interns at the cost of one experienced professional. Even if they are hired to full-time employment, their base salary will improve the overall cost of IT production.

Utilizing Contractors

Contractors are experienced IT professionals who can work for a temporary period, possess a unique skillset that is absent in existing team members, and are capable of doing the heavy lifting on a project. This type of worker is paid either hourly or daily (per diem). Their hourly rate is typically much higher than the that of the organization's permanent talent, but they work only for a limited time. The length of their contract depends on the reason they were hired. It can vary from several days to several months and can be renewed periodically if necessary. Some contractors remain at a specific organization for many years if they prove their merit and the company can afford their rate.

Unlike permanent employees, the expectation from contractors and consultants is much higher. This is because they were hired in a mission critical mode, for the completion of a time sensitive project, and because their hourly rate begins the moment they start the task. As such, contractors are burning company dollars whether or not they are being productive. Improper contractor utilization will increase the IT expenditure and lower the return on investment (ROI).

Using contractors wisely can minimize IT budget wastefulness. Only contractors who have experience in the same field under a similar business process should be considered, so they can add value to the project from day one. Even for experienced contractors, there is a period of several days where they get to know the team members and fully grasp their assignment. However, they should be productive from the moment they step foot inside the company, otherwise the organization is paying someone to do nothing. Sure, every organization has a different business strategy, but the technical work is identical across the board. When this strategy is not implemented, the contractor will spend the duration of their contract learning everything. By the time they are up to speed, it is time for them to go. This results in a huge loss for the company. This is where the importance of documentation in every regard (what, how, where, when) pays huge dividends. It allows the contractor to get up to speed in a short time and keeps the wheels of productivity turning.

Hiring Experts

Of course, experts in a given field come at a high cost. However, as mentioned above, individuals who have worked on a specific task for an extended period take less time adjusting to a new organization. They are able to jump into the company and bring productivity from the first hour they sit behind their computer. Time spent teaching employees the technical knowledge they should already possess is money that is being thrown into the garbage. The cost of using several experts benefits a company more than dozens of inexperienced workers earning a low salary. This is why managers and leaders must identify the mission-critical tasks within a project so that they know where to assign experienced personnel and where to engage junior employees and interns.

Senior, Remote Employees

Skilled employees are expensive. It is possible to save money through the use of skilled and experienced IT specialists who work from a remote location. Regardless of the level of expertise, companies pay remote employees a lower salary than those who commute to work every day. This solution benefits everyone. Remote employees are willing to accept this lower pay because of the ease of working from home, not having to get ready for work every morning, not losing time in rush hour traffic, and saving money on travel expenses. Most remote employees also appreciate the flexibility of the schedule, especially if they have children who they drop off and pick up from school every day. There is also the added benefit that very few companies are remote-friendly, so remote experts tend to remain with the same company for a long time. They appreciate the ability to spend time with their family and stay close to their spouse's job and children's school, while still engaging with the field they love. As such, hiring remote workers saves the company money because these workers expect lower wages.

Virtual Teams

Beyond reducing salary spending for on-site workers, virtual teams also allow for less management positions. Administrative workers in a common office handle a team of between seven and ten members. With a virtual team, this number can be easily adjusted to managing 20 or more. Managers earn a higher salary than normal employees, so under a structure with viable virtual team utilization, a company can save quite a bit by needing less team leaders.

Minimize Offshore Resources

Offshore is a common organizational cost-saving strategy. It is simple: workers overseas work as a lower rate than local tech experts. However, ROI calculations are not based solely on the wage of the team members. Just because management is paying a significantly less rate for jobs carried out offshore does not mean the company is guaranteed to save money. Many offshore projects result in a higher or nearly identical overall cost than projects completed domestically. For example, there may be travel costs associated with the project, such as management traveling abroad to meet with the offshore team or the offshore personnel traveling around for working purposes, so that management fails to calculate the true ROI of a given job. This cost is increased when dealing with hardware that must be shipped back and forth between locations. Overall, the cost of maintaining an offshore office paying a present market salary to the offshore worker is not cheap anymore. This is because the present salary for offshore workers is much higher than it was only a few years ago. Sure, using offshore personnel can benefit in the short-term, but should be carefully considered and avoided in most long-term situations. They should only be used, however, when necessary, and not abused for the sake of lower worker rates.

SOFTWARE DEVELOPMENT

Modern IT professionals have the choice between developing in-house, purchasing commercial off-the-shelf (COTS) software, or using an open source solution. Decisions are often made in today's technology-driven world between developing in-house or outsourcing. Regardless of the choice, there are ways to save costs in either style. This is through a conformity to and enforcement of the best practices that relate to any given project.

Development Method

Before selecting either the waterfall or agile method, team leaders should decide which works best of their employees. Through collaboration with the software developers, the pros and cons of each should be outlined. This should be repeated for any given task or project if the parameters and expectations are vastly different.

Artificial Intelligence

Managers should also evaluate whether AI is worth implementation. Machine learning has increased its sway in the software field in recent years, and there are potential benefits in nearly every type of business, organization, or field. Automation should be considered and used whenever possible. It is possible to automate all repeated work. However, careful evaluation is crucial to determine whether a given task can or should be automated. While automation can save time and energy, which reduces cost, it is not possible to automate every task.

Because of the prominence machine learning has grown into recent prominence, it is important to understand what artificial intelligence is, and what it is not. Simply put, AI means any task that a machine carries out exactly the way a human would. It is based on algorithms and can often far exceed human potential based on the computing power of the system it is running on. AI has the power to handle many tasks normally attributed to human workers, for instance problem solving and adapting to situations. Machine learning is an element of AI and uses information obtained to learn and adapt.

However, it should be noted that artificial intelligence is not all that "intelligent". Intelligence is understood to be the ability to adapt to unforeseen situations and events. AI systems do not think on their own; rather they are programmed to learn and adapt based on the algorithms. Many business processes can be automated so that they run on their own, but the AI software behind them is incapable of changing when unexpected data arises.

Although these systems are not "intelligent" in every sense of the word, they can certainly improve how businesses are run and operated and can be used to cut costs across the board because they can take on duties in place of a salaried employee. Beyond replacing workers through the automation of simple and mundane labor, machine learning can assist with implementing the ever-important big data into business operations.

Big data can be used to analyze the marketplace so that

the organization can assemble large quantities of information about customer buying histories and their overall purchasing behavior. Such data-driven marketing techniques can then predict market trends and provide leads that allow a business to grow into a new segment of potential customers. Big data can also assist in making predictions as to which direction the company should move in so that it adapts to customer needs and desires to offer the right products at the right time.

AI can also be useful in the process of organizing emails into categories such as those requiring immediate attention, those that can be put off for later, and those that can be ignored completely. This saves management quite a bit of time in going through the masses of company messages or responding to every email that comes into the inbox. This organization can also automate meeting times, other important calendar items, to-do lists, and more, essentially filling the role of a personal assistant.

Move to the Cloud

In today's Web-driven world, cloud services are more practical than ever. Many costs related to maintaining in-house servers and network equipment can be relived through cloud-based solutions. There is also less labor work related to setting up the systems and related hardware. Less hardware technicians working in an office means less money spent on staffing. It is also easier to expand the cloud requirements of more storage, memory, CPU, or communication requirements on a cloud service than making the adjustments to the company servers. The benefits of using the cloud go far beyond cost-saving.

Delivering Quality Services

Quality cannot be mentioned enough. Beyond the improvement of the company reputation (as mentioned above) for fulfilling client needs, quality assurance can also have a serious impact on spending. A project or task that was rushed to completion because of tight deadlines or inadequate staffing may seem like saving money through earning a short-term gain on schedule. However, the cost in debugging, fixing errors, and communicating progress to customers after they have received a poor-quality product will override these small profit boosts. It is entirely possible that additional contractors need to be brought in simply to solve an issue that could have been avoided during the quality assurance phase. Instead of rushing to meet deadlines, all deliverables must be properly tested, even if this means a missed projection.

SOFTWARE LICENSING

Through the use of software asset management (SAM) tools, it is possible to cut spending up to 30 percent.[14] The cost of licensing software is a major hit to the IT budget. Managers are disinclined to shift their software because the team is optimized based on the current configurations. However, there are workarounds for even the most adamant team leader. It is not easy to optimize software license automation because the process is new and has not yet garnered mainstream appeal. Still, the potential cost saving makes learning how to enact SAM tools and similar procedures in an organization a no-brainer. Through the following tips, there can be cause for celebration when the final IT spending is calculated.

License Recycling

It is possible to reduce spending by reusing software that has fallen into disuse in favor of newer, more expensive products. Many companies buy software for one specific project and then never use the program again. In this scenario, management should either look into recycling software that has already been purchased, or more importantly, truly consider whether a software license has lasting appeal before approving its purchase. All company software should be used to its maximum potential and not left in limbo as the team moves onto different projects.

Configuration Optimization

When buying software licenses, using the default configurations can cost the company untold sums of wasted spending. Although going through the setup and choosing the arrangement that works best for the given IT team takes time, the cost saving potential is enormous. Datacenter software carries the biggest weight and should be configured according to only what will be used. Budget analysts should make changes based on team recommendations and not ignore this process because buying licenses appear simple and obvious. It is neither.

SAM Tools

The above processes may be more difficult and time-consuming than the IT team can indulge. Beyond this, accurately performing them is a specialized trade that not many managers or team members possess. For these reasons, most companies would benefit from the use of a SAM (software asset management) tool that automates license optimization. Manually going through each software license can be avoided and up to 30 percent of cost can be reduced. These tools pay for themselves and more after the first year of operation.

GENERAL COST SAVING TACTICS

- **Reduce shelfware and use old tools.** Companies should get rid of any software that is not being currently used. Also, there may be many tools that were purchased during a big budget period that the company can decide it no longer needs.
- **Competition lowers costs.** Successful companies can set vendors to compete against one another for their products. In such cases, the organization can save money by

switching to a competitor. However, the team must be careful to calculate all transferable costs so they don't end up spending more money moving to a new service.

- **Telecom expense management.** Sourcing, benchmarking, negotiating, and auditing can be performed by a professional management firm. Because of the time it takes for an organization to keep track of their records, they could save anywhere from 10 to 30 percent by letting the experts take this task over.
- **Upgrade only when necessary.** Sure, IT professionals want to use the latest hardware and software. However, it is possible to stretch out the use of older machines and platforms for another year or two and save money in the upgrading process. When maintenance fees of older computers counterbalance the cost of upgrading, though, it becomes smarter to shift to newer models.
- **Cheaper hardware.** It is not always necessary to run top-of-the-line supercomputers for the company servers. Instead, one powerful PC can be linked to cheap devices to work at the same level as an expensive server unit.
- **Smart Shopping.** Hardware and software costs can quickly add up. Buying only the hardware that truly needed is one way to save money. Another way is going through all purchasing options before buying a new

product. Shopping around for sales, discounts, or making deals with vendors can pay off huge if the company spends a lot on the IT department. Refurbished hardware is also a possibility. Also, sometimes hardware can be rented instead of bought, especially if it will only be used for one or two projects.

- **Green Initiatives.** Buying environmentally safe products should be at the forefront of any company's vision. Beyond improving the organizational reputation with the promise of a greener company (information that can be added to the website), going green can save money spent on printing large amounts of documents, unsustainable lighting fixtures, and dated heating/cooling systems, among others.

- **Backup data.** If data is lost, untold amounts of money will be flushed down the drain in the recovery process. By having a backup of every important document, code, or all customer information, a potential financial disaster can be averted. As written previously in this work, in today's world, data equals money. Losing data means losing money. It is that simple.

- **Protect data.** Losing data is not only a matter of hardware failure. Hackers scour the internet to steal important information from companies. When customer data is stolen and made public, it is almost guaranteed that this customer will seek their IT services elsewhere. When company data is stolen, a competitor can overtake the market. Protecting data is imperative towards protecting a company's profitability.

TYPES OF COST SAVING

There are different ways an organization can save money. Most of the above tips fall into one of the below categories. Some are more viable than others and have a lasting effect, while many are fleeting and have a nominal impact on overall spending.

Cost Reduction

This is one of the most sought-after cost saving types because the saved money is shown clearly in the company's bottom line. Cost reduction means an organization's money is saved against the budget. Reducing the employees who work on a given project falls into this category because less salary is spent (normally this means hiring less contractors, not firing contracted team members). Optimizing spending on materials also allows a company to fall below their budgeted value. In this situation, it is possible to sell the product for less than normal and maintain the profit predictions. Of course, selling the product at the original price would only increase profit margins more.

Cost Avoidance

As understandable by the name, cost avoidance means not spending money that could have otherwise been spent. For example, a company was set to buy a new software application but then learned that they could proceed using already available solutions. Another example is not updating company hardware because it could be used for another year. This type of cost saving only impacts the bottom line if the money was already allocated to a given purchase as per the budget. Then, cost avoidance can be linked together with cost reduction.

Opportunity Cost

These cost savings are similar to cost avoidance in that money that given task or software component cannot be spent on another. Or: money for Program B is impossible because Program A is already being used. The difference here is that due to the cost saving, the allocated budget can then be distributed to another venture to enhance business opportunities. Say, for example, an excellent contractor is available, but the team already has several members who can serve that role. Then, money can be used to take the team members on an outdoor expedition, and thus, enhance morale and productivity. The contractor may then be hired on the upcoming project because it becomes unnecessary to spend money on an extracurricular activity to make employees happy. As such, opportunity costs can occur in a cyclical fashion.

Isolated Savings

This temporary saving method can also be called "one-shot profit" and it occurs across many business types. In the IT field, it can occur when redundant or unused hardware is sold for a brief gain. There is a lot of extra equipment laying around in any office than can traded to another company who will use it for a small tipping of the budget scales.

Soft Savings

In short, soft savings happen when products are delivered on time. Improvements can be made to overall performance to counteract a pattern of late deliveries, delays, and other issues such as errors that impact work as scheduled. Money is saved because the timeline is adjusted to the positive, which means products are delivered when they should be, and profit is earned earlier than last quarter. Although soft savings reflect an increase in productivity, they rarely affect the bottom line because timely delivery was in the original plan.

Carrying Cost

In a warehouse, carrying cost is defined as the financial impact of holding items in storage. For IT, this relates to the holding of a software or program code on company servers. If a product is not released, even though all of the necessary designing, development, testing, and planning has been carried out, a company is losing money. In any environment, a product is only profitable once it is being sold as intended.

Layout

It is possible to save money through maximizing the layout of an office so that employees don't waste time moving around when they need a particular product, service, or to reach another team member. However, these savings are minimal at best and can hardly be considered in a budget improvement report. It is possible to turn off unused equipment, lighting, or electronic sensors during specific hours for savings on an electricity bill. Some companies rent out unused office space to another organization to maximize their spending and earn money from something they already have in their possession. The latter is similar to the isolated savings mentioned above.

REFERENCES

[1] Collins, Jim. *Good to Great: Why Some Companies Make the Leap...and Others Don't*. New York, NY: HarperCollins Publishers, 2001.

[2] Pratt, Siofra. "Is Your Application Process Driving Away Top Talent at the Final Hurdle?" *Social Talent*, December 16, 2014.

[3] Drucker, Peter F. *The Effective Executive: The Definitive Guide to Getting the Right Things Done*. New York, NY: HarperCollins Publishers, 2006.

[4] *Corporate Responsibility Magazine*, 2018.

[5] McCunn, Lindsay J., Ph.D. "Environmental Stimulation and Environmental Psychology." *Psychology Today*, January 25, 2015.

[6] "The Anatomy of the Perfect Technical Interview from a Former Amazon VP." *First Round Review*. Accessed Summer 2018. https://firstround.com/review/The-anatomy-of-the-perfect-technical-interview-from-a-former-Amazon-VP/.

[7] Boitnott, John. "8 Unique Job Perks That Might Be Better than a Raise." *Business Insider*, May 4, 2016.

[8] CliftonStrengths | Gallup. 2018. Accessed Summer 2018. https://www.gallupstrengthscenter.com.

[9] *Project Management Body of Knowledge*. Project

Management Institute, 1996.

[10] Patton, Michael Quinn. "Evaluation, Knowledge Management, Best Practices, and High Quality Lessons Learned." *American Journal of Evaluation* 22, no. 3 (September 1, 2001): 329-36. doi:10.1177/109821400102200307.

[11] Carnegie, Dale. *How To Win Friends & Influence People*. New York, NY: Simon & Schuster, 1998.

[12] Spain, Everett, and Boris Groysberg. "Making Exit Interviews Count." *Harvard Business Review*, April 2016, 88-95.

[13] "Data Breach Investigations Report (DBIR)." *Verizon*, 2018.

[14] Marquis, Hank, Gary Spivak, and Victoria Barber. "Cut Software Spending Safely With SAM." *Gartner*, March 16, 2016.

ABOUT THE AUTHOR

Abul Mohaimin lives in New Jersey, USA with his wife, son, and daughter. His strong technological background and MBA degree helped him to achieve a blend of management, business, and technical skills. Throughout his career, he has offered consulting services to over a dozen large and mid-size American corporations. He currently works as a Senior Director at a renowned U.S. organization that provides commercial data, analytics, and insights for businesses.

Thomas J. Feliciano is a New Jersey-native who has traveled the world. Living, working, and studying across four continents, he currently resides in Istanbul, Turkey with his wife and baby daughter. He is passionate about reading, writing, learning, teaching, and professional wrestling. Working as an English teacher and freelance writer, he values expression, language, and truth.